Food Safety (General Food Hygiene) Regulations 1995

Food Safety (Temperature Control) Regulations 1995

Industry Guide to Good Hygiene Practice:

Retail Guide

Chadwick House Group Ltd.

ISBN 0 900 103 60 4

PUBLISHED BY CHADWICK HOUSE GROUP LTD.

Chadwick Court
15 Hatfields
London SE1 8DJ

Tel: 0171 827 5882 Main switchboard: 0171 827 9929 Fax: 0171 827 9930
Chadwick House Group Ltd. (CHGL) is a commercial company, wholly owned by the
Chartered Institute of Environmental Health (CIEH). The company's mission is to
provide quality products and services to create awareness and to raise standards in the
health environment and safety of the public. We intend to remain the premier
provider by continual investment in our people, products and services in support of
the aims of the CIEH. Our main activities are focused on training, communications
and conferences and exhibitions. It also markets a wide selection of books and videos
relating to environmental health. The CIEH is a professional and educational body,
founded in 1883 and dedicated to the promotion of environmental health and to
encouraging the highest possible standards in the training and the work of
environmental health officers. The Chartered Institute has over 9,000 members most of
whom work for local authorities in England, Wales and Northern Ireland. Apart from
providing services and information to members, the Institute also advises government
departments on environmental health and is consulted by them on any proposed
legislation relevant to the work of environmental health officers.
The Chartered Institute is a Registered Charity.

FOR INFORMATION:

If you need help to understand the guidance in this booklet contact your local environmental health department.

"এই পুস্তিকার নির্দেশাবলী বুঝতে যদি আপনার সাহায্যের দরকার হয়, তাহলে আপনার স্থানীয় পরিবেশ স্বাস্থ্য বিভাগ (Environmental Health Department)-এর সঙ্গে যোগাযোগ করুন।"

(Bengali)

આ નાની પુસ્તિકામાં આપેલ માર્ગદર્શન સમજવામાં તમને જો મદદની જરૂર હોય તો મહેરબાની કરીને તમારા સ્થાનિક એનવાઇરનમન્ટલ હેલ્થ ડિપાર્ટમન્ટને (પર્યાવરણજન્ય આરોગ્ય ખાતાનો) સંપર્ક સાધશો।

(Gujarati)

"ਜੇ ਤੁਹਾਨੂੰ ਇਸ ਕਿਤਾਬਚੇ ਦੀ ਰਹਿਨੁਮਾਈ ਸਮਝਣ ਵਿਚ ਮੱਦਦ ਚਾਹੀਦੀ ਹੈ ਤਾਂ ਆਪਣੇ ਸਥਾਨਕ ਐਨਵਾਇਰਨਮੈਂਟਲ ਹੈਲਥ ਡਿਪਾਰਟਮੈਂਟ (Environmental Health Department) ਨਾਲ ਸੰਪਰਕ ਕਰੋ।"

(Punjabi)

"اگر آپ کو اِس کتابچہ میں دی گئی رہنمائی کو سمجھنے میں مدد کی ضرورت ہے تو اپنے مقامی انوائرمینٹل ہیلتھ ڈپارٹمنٹ سے رابطہ قائم کیجئے"۔

(Urdu)

如果您想瞭解關於本手冊的詳細指引，請向您當地的環保處洽詢。

(Chinese)

«Αν χρειαστείτε βοήθεια στην κατανόηση των οδηγιών που περιέχονται σε αυτό το βιβλιαράκι, επικοινωνήστε με τη Διεύθυνση Περιβαλλοντικής Υγιεινής της περιοχής σας».

(Greek)

Eğer bu elkitabındaki açıklamaları anlayabilmek için yardıma ihtiyaç duyuyorsanız, yerel Çevre Sağlığı Dairenize başvurunuz.

(Turkish)

CONTENTS

Preface

This Industry Guide to good hygiene practice gives advice to retail businesses on how to comply with The Food Safety (General Food Hygiene) Regulations 1995. It also contains guidance to compliance with The Food Safety (Temperature Control) Regulations 1995 and their equivalent Regulations for Northern Ireland.

This is an official Guide to the Regulations which has been developed in accordance with Article 5 of the EC Directive on the Hygiene of Foodstuffs (93/43/EEC).

Whilst this Guide is not legally binding, Food Authorities must give its content due consideration when enforcing the Regulations. It is hoped that the information which this Guide contains will help you both to meet your legal obligations and to ensure food safety.

Acknowledgements

The British Retail Consortium is grateful to the members of the "Food Safety and Hygiene Working Group" who prepared the Guide.

Sue Cosgrove	-	Tesco
Chris Dabner	-	National Association of Master Bakers
Robin Harbach	-	Somerfield
Nigel Hayes	-	The Boots Company
David Hill	-	Kwik Save
Peter Jackson	-	Safeway
Bob Jamie	-	Scottish Grocers Federation
Bob Mitchell	-	Marks & Spencer
John Morris	-	British Retail Consortium
Janet Nunn	-	British Retail Consortium
Stephen Phillips	-	Asda
David Thurston (Chairman)	-	J Sainsbury
David Yates	-	Spar

The British Retail Consortium is also pleased to acknowledge the helpful contributions provided by:-

William Connon	-	Department of Health
Mark Du Val	-	LACOTS

In addition to the above thanks also go to all those who read and commented on the drafts.

Finally, the BRC wishes to express its gratitude to Mrs J Hardwick and Mrs S Tilney and the administrative team at Sainsbury's Group Legal Services for their work in the production of this Guide.

Introduction

This Guide has been produced by the British Retail Consortium on behalf of the retail trade and is intended to assist food shopkeepers to meet the legal requirements of The Food Safety (General Food Hygiene) Regulations 1995, The Food Safety (Temperature Control) Regulations 1995 and the equivalent Regulations for Northern Ireland. You are not legally obliged to follow this Guide and can choose other ways to meet the Regulations if you wish.

The Guide has however been formally recognised by the Secretary of State for Health. Local authority enforcement officers are required to give due consideration to its content when carrying out inspections of your business. If you follow the recommendations in the Guide it will help you meet the requirements of the Regulations and will also minimise the risk that your business will be the cause of a customer's complaint or illness.

The Regulations build on previous requirements and most well-run businesses should find that they will already meet most of the obligations in them. However, the Regulations do require businesses to look at their operations in a different way, and conduct an assessment of the risks to food safety within their business, and to apply the necessary precautions to deal with these. This is known as "HAZARD ANALYSIS".

The Guide provides the information necessary for you to do this and includes a simple assessment chart which you can complete as a record of the work you have done, to demonstrate to an enforcement officer how you have sought to comply with the Regulations.

Other regulations relating to food may also apply to your business - depending on what you sell. These regulations include compositional standards, requirements for labelling of food and temperature controls on certain frozen foods. Where practicable we have referred to these provisions in the Guide, though it was not possible to give detailed comments on their content.

Scope

This Guide is intended to apply to food retailers including:-

- GROCERS
- BUTCHERS
- FISHMONGERS
- GREENGROCERS
- DELICATESSENS
- SUPERMARKETS (including in-store bakeries)

It also applies to businesses where food is only a part of what they do such as:-

- FOOD SHOPS AT PETROL STATIONS
- NEWSAGENTS

In some cases, more specific guidance may be obtained from other guides in this series. These may be helpful to you, though it will be sufficient for you to follow the advice given here.

However, if you provide catering or operate a craft bakery you should use the Catering Guide (ISBN 0 900 103 00 0) or Baking Guide (ISBN 0 900 103 55 8) instead of the Retail Guide for those parts of your business.

How To Use The Guide

IT IS NOT INTENDED THAT ALL RETAILERS WILL HAVE TO READ THE WHOLE OF THE GUIDE. It is structured in four parts which will help you to find and apply those parts of the Regulations that are relevant to your business - depending on what you sell and how you do it.

An index is provided on Page 122.

Part 1

Provides a brief explanation of the legal background to the new Regulations. You should read this to understand what the law requires you to do.

Part 2

Provides a brief guide to the three main hazards associated with a retail food business. It is essential that you read and understand this part before trying to make an assessment of your business as the assessment chart features these three hazards.

Part 3

Comprises three charts for different categories of food you may sell and forms the basis of the assessments required by the Regulations. Careful reading of this part will help you to identify which section of the remainder of the Guide you should read and apply.

Part 4

Provides detailed guidance on each aspect of the controls needed for hygienic operation of your business.

Each section includes reference to the relevant part of the Regulations. (Pages 14-30 relate to The Food Safety (Temperature Control) Regulations 1995). Alongside you will see advice on how to comply with the requirements. Also shown is advice on good practice which goes further than the law requires and which you can follow <u>if you wish to do so</u>.

Some sections also provide further background information on the subject covered which may help you to understand it better and apply the guidance given.

At the end of each section there is a series of simple questions which you can answer to check that you understand and meet the requirements. You may show on the assessment form alongside each control whether you comply, or if not, what improvements are necessary.

Record Keeping

The Regulations DO NOT require you to keep written records of your assessment, the checklists or other areas such as temperature checks. To do so however is good practice and it will help you to demonstrate to an enforcement officer that you have sought to follow the Regulations. Section 4.11 provides further information on record keeping.

Part 1   LEGAL BACKGROUND

The law relating to food hygiene has in the past been based on providing detailed rules to be observed, but in June 1993 the European Community adopted a Directive on the Hygiene of Foodstuffs (No 93/43/EEC) to protect public health and also to try to ensure common standards of hygiene were applied throughout the EC to encourage trade in foods. The Directive is implemented in Great Britain by The Food Safety (General Food Hygiene) Regulations 1995, and in relation to temperature control by The Food Safety (Temperature Control) Regulations 1995 and similar provisions for Northern Ireland. Throughout the Guide references to the Regulations refer to the first of these except where otherwise stated.

The Directive has a number of important features:-

- 'Hygiene' is widely defined to include not only measures to ensure the safety but also measures to ensure the wholesomeness of foods. This ensures that matters such as damaged or contaminated food are also controlled.

- The Directive differs from the approach taken by previous Regulations which set down in detail how hygienic operations were to be achieved. Now there is a general obligation to ensure food is prepared, handled and sold in a hygienic way.

- The Directive requires that businesses must review their activities, identify the critical steps they need to take to ensure food safety and ensure these are properly addressed.

- A new obligation for businesses to carry out supervision and instruction and/or training for food handlers is included.

- For the first time in this area, provision is made for industry guides to be produced to assist compliance and for their recognition by Government with due consideration being given to them by Food Authorities.

There are a number of other specific regulations that relate to food hygiene, and in particular those based on other EC Legislation aimed at specific food sectors. These include fresh meat, poultry, fish products, meat products and milk but on the whole do not apply to normal retail operations. If you are packing products in a retail shop, for sale elsewhere this legislation may apply to you and in these circumstances you should approach your local enforcement officer for clarification.

Enforcement officers of the local authority have extensive powers to inspect your premises, take samples of food or materials and examine records. A summary of these is included in Appendix 1. Officers will also be pleased to provide advice and assistance to businesses on how to comply with legal requirements.

It is a criminal offence to fail to meet the requirements of the Regulations, or to have food for sale which is unfit, contaminated or may injure a person's health. If prosecuted you can be fined and in serious cases could be imprisoned and/or have your business closed down and be personally banned from running a food business in future.

Just as importantly though you may cause your customers to become seriously ill and in this case they may also be able to claim damages from you or your insurers.

Part 2   FOOD HAZARDS

> "A proprietor of a food business shall ensure that any of the following operations, namely, the preparation, processing, manufacturing, packaging, storing, transportation, distribution, handling and offering for sale or supply, of food are carried out in a hygienic way".
> (Regulation 4[1])

If a good standard of food hygiene is maintained throughout the food chain, including by the retailer, customers can be confident that the food they eat will be safe and they will not suffer any ill effects. Food hazards can occur at any stage during manufacture, storage, distribution or retail.

A hazard is anything that could cause harm to the consumer and can be grouped into three categories:-

1.   Microbiological Contamination
2.   Physical/Chemical Contamination
3.   Physical Damage

Microbiological Contamination

Micro-organisms include bacteria, viruses, yeasts and moulds. They are very small and generally can only be seen under a microscope but they are present almost everywhere. Not all micro-organisms are harmful, however, and some are essential in the manufacture of food products such as cheese and yogurt or for brewing beers.

Bacteria

These are the most important micro-organisms in terms of hazard to the consumer. Contamination of foodstuffs by certain types can cause illness or even death due to food poisoning. Food poisoning occurs when a person eats a food contaminated with bacteria that has either produced a poison (toxin) or has grown to sufficiently large numbers and itself causes illness. The body reacts to the toxin or bacteria and will try to get rid of them, resulting in the symptoms of food poisoning which may include:-

Diarrhoea	Vomiting
Stomach Pains	Sweating
Headache	Collapse

The elderly, the very young, in some cases pregnant women and those who are already unwell are particularly vulnerable and in severe cases death may occur.

Bacteria grow in number by dividing into two. In order to grow and divide bacteria need favourable conditions.

- Food   -   e.g. meat, milk, cereals, vegetables or food debris.

- Water   -   bacteria will not grow in totally dry conditions, though moisture in the air will be sufficient to allow growth.

- Warmth -   most bacteria require warmth to grow, normally between 8°C and 63°C. Growth will be very slow below 8°C or over 63°C for most types.

● Time - division can occur every few minutes if the correct environ mental conditions are available and within a very short time they can multiply to levels which can cause poisoning.

To avoid the hazard of food poisoning from bacteria you must both ensure that food is safe in the first place and also avoid the conditions which allow any bacteria which are present to grow in number.

In the retail environment food may be contaminated by bacteria from various sources:

● By coughing, sneezing or spitting over food.

● Hands - cuts, skin infections. Not washing hands after going to the lavatory or handling refuse. By touching the nose, mouth, ears or hair where bacteria are always present.

● Cross Contamination - raw foods such as meat or vegetables carry bacteria which may be transferred to and grow on cooked and ready to eat foods.

● Pests, Animals - insects, rodents and pets all carry bacteria which may be transferred to foods by direct or indirect contact.

It is usually impossible to tell if food has been contaminated by food poisoning bacteria or their toxins. It is not possible to see, smell or taste any difference between contaminated and wholesome food. Thus it is vital to protect food from bacterial contamination at every stage and to control growing conditions.

Certain bacteria may also cause food spoilage and these types are found in the air, soil and sometimes water. They cause discoloration, slime and odour. Meat and fish are often spoiled this way. These bacteria can grow at low temperatures so good hygiene standards are essential to avoid contamination.

Viruses

Certain viruses can cause illness by being carried on food. They cannot multiply and grow on food but may be transported with it from person to person. They will be destroyed by thorough cooking but ready to eat foods handled by an infected person may cause illness to the consumer.

Yeasts and Moulds

These are often useful for the production of foods such as bread, beer and 'blue' cheeses. They can, however, cause food spoilage and may even result in toxins being formed in foods. Evidence of mould growth in food preparation areas or on foods indicate poor cleaning and food safety practices.

Contamination by yeasts, moulds and spoilage bacteria and subsequent growth will render most food unfit for sale.

Physical/Chemical Contamination

This is the contamination of food by any article or substance which should not be there and is not part of the normal food product.

The most common kind of physical contamination is that of foreign objects. If prepared foods or ingredients are left unprotected at any stage they are exposed to the risk of unwanted objects entering the product.

This may arise as a consequence of:

Pest control problems (insects, mouse droppings, feathers).

Equipment or maintenance failures (broken glass, nuts and bolts).

Poor personal hygiene (hair, buttons, hairgrips, fingernails, coins or plasters).

Careless cleaning (scouring pads, debris).

Poor food handling (open foods being mixed).

Most foreign objects will not cause food to decompose or deteriorate in any other way but they can cause injury. It is an offence to sell food affected by physical contamination.

Chemical contamination of foods usually occurs as a result of cleaning materials being incorrectly used or being spilled accidentally. The use of appropriate cleaning materials and good cleaning practices should avoid this.

Other contamination may arise from incorrect storage. Metal containers may go rusty and thereby contaminate the contents. Some foods such as chocolate or eggs may be tainted if stored next to other products with a strong odour.

Some people have particular sensitivity to certain foods, which in the case of nuts can be fatal. A special form of contamination is therefore where such ingredients find their way inadvertently into other foods. Special care needs to be taken to deal with this hazard as very small quantities can cause the adverse reaction. More information on this hazard can be obtained from The Anaphylaxis Campaign (Address in Appendix V).

Physical Damage

If food or its packaging is damaged this may allow bacteria or foreign objects to enter the product and cause deterioration. This is particularly hazardous where special packaging such as vacuum packs or cans have been used. In these cases damage will rapidly lead to products becoming unfit to eat.

Physical damage may also alter the quality of foods, such as bruising to fruit and vegetables which in turn can make them more susceptible to attack by moulds or pests.

Part 3   HAZARD ANALYSIS

The legal requirement to carry out Hazard Analysis is the key to the Regulations and reflects the new approach to dealing with food hygiene. It requires a retail business to examine its own operation and identify the controls necessary depending on the risk posed by the products sold.

In the Guide we have sought to provide an easy to follow way by which a retailer can carry out a self assessment.

The legal obligation is stated in Regulation 4(3) of the Regulations.

"A proprietor of a food business shall identify any step in the activities of the food business which is critical to ensuring food safety and ensure that adequate safety procedures are identified, implemented, maintained and reviewed on the basis of the following principles -

(a)   analysis of the potential food hazards in a food business operation;

(b)   identification of the points in those operations where food hazards may occur;

(c)   deciding which of the points identified are critical to ensuring food safety ("critical points");

(d)   identification and implementation of effective control and monitoring procedures at those critical points; and

(e)   review of the analysis of food hazards, the critical points and the control and monitoring procedures periodically, and whenever the food business's operations change."

Section a)   requires an understanding of the hazards that can affect a retail business, these have been fully explained in Part 2 of this Guide. We have identified three main hazards; microbiological contamination, physical/chemical contamination and physical damage.

Section b)   requires that the business must examine their own operations and establish where the hazards can occur. This not only means physical location, but also where within a process or operation a hazard can occur or be introduced.

Section c)   requires the business to decide which of the specific hazards they have identified in their own operation are critical. Critical means that if these are not controlled there is likely to be a risk to food safety. This Guide seeks to help you to do this using the assessment table.

Section d)   requires that a method of controlling and monitoring the "critical" points is both identified and used.

Section e)   requires that the situation is reviewed if the food business's operations change or if new products or equipment are introduced and on a periodic basis as a matter of course.

The following tables represent the mechanism we have devised to assist the retail business through sections (a) to (e) of Regulation 4(3).

How to Use the Assessment Tables

Step 1

To begin with you need to identify the "risk category" of foods you sell using the guidance/examples in Column A. The foods are grouped into three "risk categories".

- High Risk Foods/Foods Prepared, Produced on Site

- Medium Risk Foods

- Low Risk Foods/Fully Preserved Foods

This refers to the risk that the foods may cause illness if contaminated or allowed to deteriorate and depends upon many factors such as whether they are ready-to-eat or will be cooked first. The foods shown are only examples and are not intended to be exhaustive.

Step 2

Put a tick in Column B against the types of products you sell using the examples from Column A. If you sell <u>any</u> of the foods within a risk category then that table applies to you. The highest risk category applicable to you will be the one for which you go on and complete the Assessments.

Step 3

Column C explains the three basic hazards for the relevant risk category of business you belong to.

Step 4

Column D identifies and briefly describes the critical controls that must be applied to deal with the hazards. These controls are ones which, if not followed, will result in a high risk of the hazard occurring. **These have been listed in a priority order to deal with the hazards as effectively as possible.** Shown next to each control is a reference to the main section of the text in Part 4. Each of these must be addressed if the requirements of the Regulations are to be met.

Step 5

For each identified Critical Control there is a control measure title (Column E) and reference (Column F) for you to find the detailed information contained within Part 4 of the Guide. Each relevant section in Part 4 should be read.

Step 6

Using the advice on compliance and checklists if desired within each Part 4 section you should be able to determine whether your existing controls are adequate. If not you should identify any areas needing improvement.

Step 7

It may be helpful if any deficiencies and the improvements you need to take are then noted in Column G of the Assessment Table and realistic timescales within Column H. Column H can then be used to track your progress as each task is completed.

A completed Assessment Table can provide an ideal document to discuss with your enforcement officer on an inspection of your premises.

Food Safety (General Food Hygiene) Regulations 1995 – Guide to compliance by Retailers

Note: Having completed your assessment, should any details of your process or products change you will need to repeat these steps.

In addition to the above steps which will apply to all retailers, the Regulations also impose requirements which may or may not apply to your particular business.

If you are involved in transporting foods, including collection from wholesalers or markets you should check Section 4.14.

If your business uses mobile or temporary premises check Section 4.15.

If you use vending machines check Section 4.16.

ASSESSMENT TABLE 1 - HIGH RISK FOODS

HIGH RISK FOODS (A)	WHAT AM I SELLING? (B)	HAZARDS (C)	CRITICAL CONTROLS (D)	CONTROL MEASURES (E)	REF (F)	IMPROVEMENTS NEEDED (G)	ASSESSMENT DATE/BY (H)
FOODS MANUFACTURED / PRODUCED ON SITE - sandwiches, pizza, cakes & salads, roast chicken and other hot foods. **COOKED PRODUCTS** - containing meat, fish, eggs, cheese, cereals, pulses, vegetables, cooked poultry, cold cooked meats. Cooked bean salads. Meat and fish pate. Scotch eggs, pork pies with gelatine added after cooking. Quiches, open or lattice topped savoury pies. Sandwich fillings. **COOKED PRODUCTS INTENDED FOR FURTHER TREATMENT BEFORE EATING** - meat, fish or chicken pies, pizzas & ready made meals, partly cooked sausage rolls. Fresh pasta with meat or fish filling. e.g., ravioli. **SMOKED OR CURED MEATS** - sliced / cut after smoking or curing, e.g. cured coated hams or salamis & other fermented (continental style) sausages. **SMOKED OR CURED FISH** - whole & sliced after smoking or curing e.g. salmon, mackerel, trout, haddock & kippers. **DAIRY BASED DESSERTS** - fromage frais, mousses, creme caramels, whipped cream desserts, cream cakes. **CHEESE** - ripened soft or moulded cheeses e.g. Brie, Danish Blue, Roquefort, Camembert, Dolcelatte. **PREPARED VEGETABLE SALADS** - including those containing fruit, coleslaw, rice salads.		**Microbiological Contamination** Harmful bacteria & viruses can sometimes get into foods either in the ingredients, making up the foods, during handling, preparation & packaging, or after preparation during transport & storage. The bacteria may grow rapidly on the food if it is not refrigerated & then cause illness when it is consumed. Alternatively the bacteria may lie dormant causing a hazard only if product temperature is allowed to rise at a later time. **Physical Contamination** If prepared food or ingredients are left uncovered or unprotected during handling it is possible for foreign objects to cause contamination. Items such as pieces of packaging, hairclips or jewellery may fall into containers of food. Their presence may constitute an offence and lead to serious injury or complaints. **Physical Damage** Damage to vacuum packs, bags and protective packaging can result in opportunities for bacterial contamination and reduction in product safety or shelf life.	**Microbiological Contamination** 1. Temperature control at all times in transport, storage & display. 2. Suitably skilled and knowledgeable staff aware of risks & prevention measures. 3. Good staff hygiene to prevent bacteria transferring from them to the food. 4. Proper product shelf life/stock rotation to ensure microbiological safety & quality. 5. Suitable premises and equipment so as not to harbour bacteria & dirt, and which facilitate cleaning routines. 6. Rapid transfer of chilled products at each stage of the distribution chain. 7. Adequate cleaning to remove sources of contamination / harbourage for bacteria. 8. Extra precautions where open food is involved. 9. Pest control to avoid bacteria being transmitted by insects & rodents. 10. Monitoring of temperatures. 11. Correct disposal of waste to avoid contamination of food for sale. 12. Procedures to be in place if refrigeration equipment fails. **Physical Contamination** 1. Extra precautions for display of open foods. 2. Correct handling of products to avoid contamination from persons, premises or general environment. 3. Good staff hygiene to avoid contamination from hair, jewellery, clothing etc. 4. Good cleaning systems to prevent debris & contamination from the cleaning activity. Proper control of cleaning chemicals. 5. Pest control to prevent contamination from insects or rodents. 6. Good waste disposal to avoid increased risk of infestation. 7. Suitably skilled and knowledgeable staff aware of risks & prevention measures. **Physical Damage** 1. Correct handling to avoid damage to container or product. 2. Pest control to prevent damage to container or product by insects & rodents. 3. Suitably skilled and knowledgeable staff aware of risks & prevention measures. 4. Storage equipment & facilities such as not to put product at risk of damage. 5. Stock rotation. 6. Extra precautions for open foods. 7. Procedures for disposing of damaged foods.	Temperature Control Supervision and Instruction and/or Training Personal Hygiene Stock Rotation Structural Equipment & Facilities Product Handling Cleaning Display of Open Food Pest Control Monitoring/Records Waste Disposal Emergency Procedures Display of Open Food Product Handling Personal Hygiene Cleaning Pest Control Waste Disposal Supervision and Instruction and/or Training Product Handling Pest Control Supervision and Instruction and/or Training Equipment & Facilities Stock Rotation Display of Open Foods Waste Disposal	4.1 4.7 4.5 4.3 4.10 4.9 4.2 4.4 4.6 4.8 4.11 4.12 4.13 4.6 4.2 4.5 4.4 4.8 4.12 4.7 4.2 4.8 4.7 4.9 4.3 4.6 4.12		

ASSESSMENT TABLE 3 - LOW RISK FOODS

FULLY PRESERVED FOODS/LOW RISK FOODS (A)	WHAT AM I SELLING? (B)	HAZARDS (C)	CRITICAL CONTROLS (D)	CONTROL MEASURES (E)	REF (F)	IMPROVEMENTS NEEDED (G)	ASSESSMENT DATE/BY (H)
Foods preserved by a process of heating and packed in hermetically sealed containers while still in the container, such as canned foods, long-life ready-meals.		**Microbiological Contamination** Most of these products will not be susceptible to food poisoning organisms while in their normal state. Spoilage organisms such as yeasts and moulds may grow if shelf life is not observed.	**Microbiological Contamination** 1. Stock rotation to ensure quality and safety. 2. Extra requirements where open food is involved. (NB This includes personal hygiene). 3. Staff to be aware of risks and how to prevent them. 4. Pest control to avoid bacteria transmitted insects/rodents. 5. The right equipment and facilities to enable correct temperature maintenance for frozen foods.	Stock Rotation Display of Open Foods Personal Hygiene Supervision and Instruction and/or Training Pest Control Temperature Control	4.3 4.6 4.5 4.7 4.8 4.1		
Dried vegetables. Packet soups. Pickled foods. Preserves and jams. Dry pasta. Dry pudding mixes or dry mixes for the preparation of beverages. Chocolate and sugar confectionery. Bread and biscuits. Cakes or pastries (not containing cream or custard). Ice cream. Frozen foods.		**Physical Contamination** Any open or unwrapped foods could be contaminated by packaging materials or other foreign objects during handling & display.	**Physical Contamination** 1. Extra requirements for display of open foods. 2. Good cleaning systems to prevent debris & contamination from the cleaning activity. 3. Correct handling of product to avoid contamination from persons, premises or general environment. 4. Sufficient standard of equipment & adequate cleaning facilities. 5. Stock rotation to avoid increased risk of infestation. 6. Staff to be aware of risks and how to prevent them. 7. Sound structure such as not to harbour dirt.	Display of Open Foods Cleaning Handling Procedures Equipment & Facilities Stock Rotation Supervision and Instruction and/or Training Structure	4.6 4.4 4.2 4.9 4.3 4.7 4.10		
		Physical Damage Any damage to the packaging of these products may result in an increased risk of microbiological or physical contamination. Dented tins, squashed /split packets for example could allow metal contamination or taints to occur, or spillage from one pack onto others could occur. Incorrect storage, cold or damp environments may also physically alter product quality.	**Physical Damage** 1. Correct handling to avoid damage to container or product. 2. Storage equipment and facilities such as not to put product at risk of damage. 3. Extra requirements for open foods. 4. Staff to be aware of risks and how to prevent them.	Handling Procedures Equipment & Facilities Display of Open Foods Supervision and Instruction and/or Training	4.2 4.9 4.6 4.7		

ASSESSMENT TABLE 2 - MEDIUM RISK FOODS

MEDIUM RISK FOODS (A)	WHAT AM I SELLING? (B)	HAZARDS (C)	CRITICAL CONTROLS (D)	CONTROL MEASURES (E)	REF (F)	IMPROVEMENTS NEEDED (G)	ASSESSMENT DATE/BY (H)
Hard cheeses Cream or curd cheese Cottage cheese Non-dairy cream cakes Unripened soft cheeses Whole smoked or cured meat Fruit pies Raw meats and raw fish Sausages, bacon Fresh milk Vegetables Fruit		**Microbiological Contamination** May result in spoilage or harmful bacteria and moulds growing in or on these products. Growth may not be rapid but safety and quality considerations will reduce shelf life. Bacteria may grow after heating or thawing. **Physical Contamination** May occur from dirt, debris, loose packaging. Any open foods must be protected from foreign objects falling into or onto the product. **Physical Damage** Physical damage to the product or packaging may render it substandard to the customer. Whether by mechanical injury or incorrect storage e.g. damp environments. The appearance and quality of certain products may be severely affected by bruising e.g. fruit & vegetables.	**Microbiological Contamination** 1. Good staff hygiene to prevent bacteria transferring to the food. 2. Temperature control when required in transport, storage & display. 3. Correct handling to ensure rapid transfer between chilled conditions. 4. Suitably skilled and knowledgeable staff aware of risks and prevention measures. 5. Stock rotation to prevent microbiological spoilage beyond shelf life. 6. Adequate cleaning to remove sources of contamination/harbourage of bacteria. 7. Pest control to avoid bacteria being transmitted by insects & rodents. 8. The right equipment & facilities to enable correct temperatures, cleaning etc. 9. Extra precautions where open food is involved. 10. A sound structure such as not to harbour bacteria and dirt. **Physical Contamination** 1. Extra requirements for display of open food. 2. Correct handling of product to avoid contamination from persons, premises or general environment. 3. Good staff hygiene to avoid contamination from hair, jewellery, clothing etc. 4. Pest control to prevent contamination from insects or rodents. 5. Sufficient standard of equipment and adequate cleaning facilities. 6. Good cleaning systems to prevent debris & contamination from the cleaning activity. 7. Suitably skilled and knowledgeable staff aware of risks and prevention measures. 8. Good waste disposal to avoid contamination of food for sale. 9. Procedures for dealing with emergencies. **Physical Damage** 1. Correct handling to avoid damage to container or product. 2. Pest control to prevent damage to container or product by insects and rodents. 3. Suitably skilled and knowledgeable staff aware of risks and prevention measures. 4. Storage equipment and facilities such as not to put product at risk of damage. 5. Stock rotation. 6. Extra requirements for open foods.	Personal Hygiene Temperature Control Product Handling Supervision and Instruction and/or Training Stock Rotation Cleaning Pest Control Equipment & Facilities Display of Open Foods Structural Display of Open Foods Product Handling Personal Hygiene Pest Control Equipment & Facilities Cleaning Supervision and Instruction and/or Training Waste Disposal Emergency Procedures Product Handling Pest Control Supervision and Instruction and/or Training Equipment & Facilities Stock Rotation Display of Open Foods	4.5 4.1 4.2 4.7 4.3 4.4 4.8 4.9 4.6 4.10 4.6 4.2 4.5 4.8 4.9 4.4 4.7 4.12 4.13 4.2 4.8 4.7 4.9 4.3 4.6		

Part 4   CONTROL MEASURES

This Guide has been arranged in subject order rather than in the order of the Regulations themselves. If you are looking for guidance on a particular Regulation you can use the index in Appendix VI to find it.

4.1   TEMPERATURE CONTROL

Introduction

The control of temperature is essential in restricting the growth in numbers of bacteria and thus minimising the risk of food poisoning. For high risk foods in particular, keeping them chilled or hot is the single most important control in ensuring their safety.

As described in Part 2, bacteria need warmth to live and multiply. Generally, at temperatures of less than 8°C or more than 63°C their growth is very slow. The range between these two temperatures is known as the danger-zone where bacteria will grow rapidly and therefore it is necessary to avoid keeping foods at these temperatures.

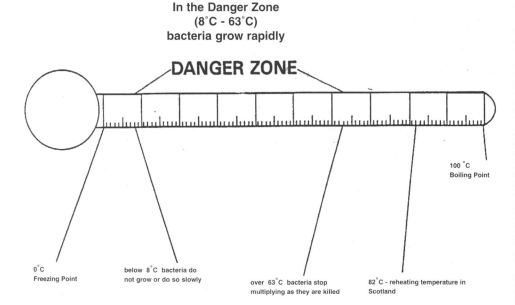

In the Danger Zone
(8°C - 63°C)
bacteria grow rapidly

DANGER ZONE

100 °C
Boiling Point

0°C
Freezing Point

below 8°C bacteria do
not grow or do so slowly

over 63°C bacteria stop
multiplying as they are killed

82°C - reheating temperature in
Scotland

The requirements of the Directive relating to temperature control have been enacted in the UK by The Food Safety (Temperature Control) Regulations 1995 rather than The Food Safety (General Food Hygiene) Regulations 1995, to which this Guide generally refers.

The temperature control Regulations make a distinction between England and Wales (with similar provision repeated for Northern Ireland) and for Scotland, where historically different rules have applied.

It is important to remember that other legislation may affect the temperature at which food can be kept. The most important of these Regulations are those that cover the hygiene of specific products such as fresh meat, meat products, poultry and game, fish and certain shellfish, dairy products and eggs. They ordinarily do not apply at retail level. For any retailers who process or pack such foods for sale off the premises it is suggested that specialist advice be sought or your EHO consulted.

Frozen foods pose a low risk provided they are kept frozen solid. Certain frozen foods may be marked 'Quick Frozen' and for these, specific temperature controls are provided in the Quick Frozen Foodstuffs Regulations 1990.

Further guidance on the storage and handling of frozen foods is available in a guide produced by the Refrigerated Food Industry Confederation.

Provisions Applicable to England, Wales and Northern Ireland

Legal requirement	Guide to compliance	Advice on good practice
temperature control Regulation 10 (1) *Subject to paragraph (2), no person shall in the course of the activities of a food business keep foodstuffs which are -* *a) raw materials, ingredients, intermediate products or finished products; and* *b) likely to support the growth of pathogenic micro-organisms or the formation of toxins, at temperatures which would result in a risk to health.*	This is the general requirement to keep certain foods at temperatures which do not result in a risk to health. Other Regulations below go on to further explain this requirement. It is important to note that not all foodstuffs are affected. Whether any particular food is caught by the Regulation will depend upon factors such as its shelf-life, composition, acidity level and method of processing or packing. As a general rule however you should consider a food to be covered by this Regulation if :- a) It is listed in column A of Assessment Table 1 (High Risk Foods) in Part 3 of this Guide, or b) It is labelled with a "use by" form of durability indication. Nevertheless, regard should be had to the above factors in deciding whether any particular food is covered by the Regulation. See also Page 18, 19 in relation to raw meat, fish and poultry. Such foods are referred to in this section as relevant foods.	Some foods such as long-life milk may be specially made so as <u>not</u> to require refrigeration. Other foods such as butter may be labelled or described as requiring refrigeration for quality purposes rather than for food safety.
temperature control Regulation 10 (2) *Consistent with food safety, limited periods outside temperature control are permitted where necessary to accommodate the practicalities of handling during preparation, transport, storage, display and service of food.*	Limited periods outside of temperature control are permitted during preparation, display, storage or transport provided that the temperature attained by the food and the time it is kept out of temperature control are not such as to pose a risk to food safety. Further guidance to this requirement is provided on Pages 20 & 21 for Regulation 7.	Periods out of temperature control and foodstuffs affected should be kept to a minimum.

Provisions Applicable to England, Wales and Northern Ireland

Legal requirement	Guide to compliance	Advice on good practice
temperature control Regulation 10 (3) *A person may contravene paragraph (1) notwithstanding that he complies with the requirements of regulations 4 and 8, and in particular the keeping of perishable foodstuffs at above a maximum storage temperature recommended in any special storage conditions for them may be in contravention of paragraph (1) notwithstanding that they are kept at a temperature of 8°C or below.*	There may be some cases where the normal maximum temperature of 8°C will not be cold enough. Foods affected will ordinarily be marked with the lower required storage temperature which must be observed provided it is necessary for the safety of the food.	Occasionally some products may be marked with a temperature of less than 8°C to protect their quality and/or shelf life. Manufacturers' advice should be sought however, before departing from the stated storage conditions.
temperature control Regulation 4 (1) *Subject to paragraph (2) and regulation 5, no person shall keep any food -* *a) which is likely to support the growth of pathogenic micro-organisms or the formation of toxins; and* *b) with respect to which any commercial operation is being carried out,* *at or in food premises at a temperature above 8°C.*	This Regulation builds upon the general provision above and specifies a maximum temperature of 8°C for relevant foods. The guidance above for foods covered is also applicable here. These foods must be kept at or below 8°C at all times except where they are covered by an exemption below. Note: It is the temperature of the food itself that is controlled and not that of the cabinet/store in which the food may be placed. (See Appendix II).	It is good practice to store high risk open foods at temperatures below 8°C if to do so is practicable and will not affect their quality.
temperature control Regulation 4 (2) *Paragraph (1) shall not apply to any food which, as part of a mail order transaction, is being conveyed by post or by a private or common carrier to an ultimate consumer.*	All foods supplied to consumers by mail order are exempt from the 8°C requirement but relevant foods must still be conveyed at a temperature which does not give rise to a risk to health, or be otherwise exempt under Regulation 5.	Relevant foods should not be supplied mail order without obtaining specialist advice/consulting your Trade Association or EHO. Any products to be supplied by mail order should be packaged in such a way that they do not become damaged or open to contamination in the course of transit.

Food Safety (Temperature Control) Regulations 1995 – Guide to compliance by Retailers

Provisions Applicable to England, Wales and Northern Ireland

Legal requirement	Guide to compliance	Advice on good practice
temperature control Regulation 4 (3) *Subject to regulation 5, no person shall supply by mail order any food which -* *(a) is likely to support the growth of pathogenic micro-organisms or the formation of toxins; and* *(b) is being or has been conveyed by post or by a private or common carrier to an ultimate consumer,* *at a temperature which has given rise to or is likely to give rise to a risk to health.*		
temperature control Regulation 5 *Regulation 4 shall not apply to -* *a) food which -* *i) has been cooked or reheated,* *ii) is for service or on display for sale, and* *iii) needs to be kept hot in order to control the growth of pathogenic micro-organisms or the formation of toxins;*	This Regulation provides for exemption from the 8°C temperature requirement of Regulation 4. a) relates to food intended to be sold hot. This is covered by Regulation 8.	
b) food which, for the duration of its shelf life, may be kept at ambient temperatures with no risk to health;	Some perishable foods may be kept at room (ambient) temperatures as they will not support growth of pathogens. These include margarines, butter and fats (though not low-fat spreads) and most jams, pickles and prepared sauces whilst packaging is intact. Manufacturer's / supplier's advice must be sought if in doubt. Other perishable foods may also be kept at ambient temperatures if the shelf-life is adjusted accordingly so as not to pose a risk to health. Uncut baked egg custards or curd tarts can be kept at ambient temperature for up to 24 hours after production. Cooked pies and pasties (provided nothing has been added to them after cooking) and sausage rolls can similarly be kept at ambient temperature on the day of production and the day after.	For perishable foods having a short shelf life it is nevertheless good practice to keep them refrigerated.

Provisions Applicable to England, Wales and Northern Ireland

Legal requirement	Guide to compliance	Advice on good practice
	Sandwiches and cream cakes can be kept at ambient temperature for up to 4 hours after production.	It is good practice to refrigerate sandwiches and cream cakes if not for immediate sale.
	For time exemptions, a method must be adopted to ensure the periods specified are followed. At the end of the period products must be disposed of.	The use of stickers or coloured wraps may be helpful.
temperature control *Regulation 5*		
(c) food which is being or has been subjected to a process such as dehydration or canning intended to prevent the growth of pathogenic micro-organisms at ambient temperatures, but this paragraph shall cease to apply in circumstances where - *(i) after or by virtue of that process the food was contained in a hermetically sealed container, and* *(ii) that container has been opened;*	Most canned or similarly packed foods will not require refrigeration until opened. Some large cans of meats may not be fully sterilised in which case the labelling will say so. These must be kept chilled even if unopened. Once opened, or rehydrated, product must be removed from its packaging and placed in a suitable clean container. Temperature control must be observed.	Canned meats may be refrigerated to aid slicing when opened. Pre-cooling will also ensure that opened product will be at the correct temperature immediately it is put on display. It is good practice to label the container with contents and date of opening or disposal.
(d) food which must be ripened or matured at ambient temperatures, but this paragraph shall cease to apply once the process of ripening or maturation is completed;	This applies principally to mould ripened cheeses such as brie, camembert and stilton. They are usually supplied ready ripened and should be kept at 8°C or less immediately.	Ripening product should be kept separately, clearly identified and marked with an indication of when ripening is complete.
(e) raw food intended for further processing (which includes cooking) before human consumption, but only if that processing, if undertaken correctly, will render that food fit for human consumption;	This provision applies eg: to raw fish and raw meat provided it is not intended to be eaten without further processing eg: meat for steak tartare which must be kept at or less than 8°C. In other cases it can be assumed that meat will be cooked properly. Certain types of fish such as mackerel and tuna are not covered by this provision.	It is good practice to limit the amount of raw meat on ambient display, and to keep stocks chilled. Raw fish should be kept in storage and on display for sale at the temperature of melting ice. This can be achieved by placing the fish in/on a bed of crushed ice. Good contact between ice and fish should be maintained.

Food Safety (Temperature Control) Regulations 1995 – Guide to compliance by Retailers

Provisions Applicable to England, Wales and Northern Ireland

Legal requirement	Guide to compliance	Advice on good practice
temperature control Regulation 5 *(f) food to which Council Regulation (EEC) No 1906/90 on certain marketing standards for poultry, as amended, applies;* *(g) food to which Council Regulation (EEC) No 1907/90 on certain marketing standards for eggs, as amended, applies.*	Although exempt from the requirement of Regulation 4, the EC Regulation requires fresh poultry meat (chicken, duck, goose, turkey and guinea fowl) to be kept and/or displayed for sale at temperatures not exceeding 4°C or less than -2°C. Regulation 4 does not apply to eggs. The EC Regulation does not impose any temperature control requirement for eggs in shell at retail level.	It is good practice to avoid excess heat, or large changes in temperature for eggs in shell.
temperature control Regulation 6 (1) *In any proceedings for an offence of contravening regulation 4 (1), it shall be a defence for a person charged (for the purposes of this regulation called "the defendant") to prove that -* *(a) a food business responsible for manufacturing, preparing or processing the food has recommended that it is kept -* *(i) at or below a specified temperature between 8°C and ambient temperatures, and* *(ii) for a period not exceeding a specified shelf-life;* *(b) that recommendation has, unless the defendant is that food business, been communicated to the defendant either by means of a label on the packaging of the food or by means of some other appropriate form of written instruction;* *(c) the food was not kept by the defendant at a temperature above the specified temperature; and* *(d) at the time of the commission of the alleged offence, the specified shelf-life had not been exceeded.*	This Regulation allows a manufacturer or processor of food to recommend that his product can be kept at a temperature higher than 8°C for a specified shelf-life. A retailer who follows a manufacturer's advice in these circumstances will not be in breach of Regulation 4. Where a supplier makes a recommendation permitting a temperature higher than 8°C, there is no obligation to keep foods at that temperature and the retailer can choose to keep it instead at 8°C or less with other products. The shelf-life recommended must however still be observed. Where a retailer has foods with different temperature requirements kept together in the same cabinet, it is necessary that the cabinet operates at the lowest temperature required for the foods stored there.	

Provisions Applicable to England, Wales and Northern Ireland

Legal requirement	Guide to compliance	Advice on good practice
temperature control Regulation 6 (2)		
(2) A food business responsible for manufacturing, preparing or processing food shall not recommend that any food is kept - *(a) at or below a specified temperature between 8˚C and ambient temperatures; and*	A manufacturer, or producer seeking to make a recommendation for a greater than 8℃ temperature/shelf-life combination must conduct a proper scientific assessment to ensure that the recommendation does not result in any risk to health.	It is recommended that retailers who may produce products for others should not make such recommendations without independent scientific advice.
(b) for a period not exceeding a specified shelf-life, unless that recommendation is supported by a well-founded scientific assessment of the safety of the food at the specified temperature.	The Department of Health has provided further guidance on scientific assessments in their Guidance to the Regulations.	
temperature control Regulation 7 (1)		
In any proceedings for an offence of contravening regulation 4(1), it shall be a defence for a person charged to prove that the food - *(a) was for service or on display for sale;*	This regulation allows for an exemption from the requirement to keep relevant food at 8℃ or less for foods which are displayed for sale for a single period of not more than 4 hours.	The use of stickers, coloured wraps or similar methods to make clear to employees when food is to be removed from display.
(b) had not previously been kept for service or on display for sale at a temperature above 8˚C or, in appropriate circumstances, the recommended temperature; and	Care must be taken to ensure that the time period can be properly observed.	The practice of topping up ambient displays throughout a day risks breaching the 4 hour period and should be avoided.
(c) had been kept for service or on display for sale for a period of less than four hours.	Food must be disposed of at the end of the 4 hour period unless the retailer is confident that it remains wholesome, in which case it must be chilled quickly to 8℃ or less and sold/disposed of within a period which does not pose a risk to health.	The amount of food kept for service or display out of refrigeration should be kept to the minimum necessary.

Legal requirement	Guide to compliance	Advice on good practice
temperature control Regulation 7 (2) *In any proceedings for an offence of contravening regulation 4(1), it shall be a defence for the person charged to prove that the food - (a) was being transferred -* *(i) to a vehicle used for the purposes of the activities of a food business from, or* *(ii) from a vehicle used for the purposes of the activities of a food business to,* *premises (which includes vehicles) at which the food was going to be kept at or at below 8 °C or, in appropriate circumstances, the recommended temperature; or* *(b) was kept at a temperature above 8 °C or, in appropriate circumstances, the recommended temperature for an unavoidable reason, such as -* *(i) to accommodate the practicalities of handling during and after processing or preparation,* *(ii) the defrosting of equipment, or* *(iii) temporary breakdown of equipment,* *and was kept at a temperature above 8 °C or, in appropriate circumstances, the recommended temperature for a limited period only and that period was consistent with food safety.*	This Regulation provides a defence for contravening Regulation 4(1), by allowing relevant food to exceed 8°C or, if appropriate, a recommended temperature as described in Regulation 6. The circumstances however are limited to transfers to or from vehicles or for an unavoidable reason such as handling or preparation, defrosting or temporary breakdown of equipment. No time is specified but the period above 8°C must be limited in such a way as to ensure the food is not allowed to pose a risk to health. The time will depend on the type of food and the temperature attained, but a single period of up to two hours at ambient temperature can be considered acceptable for any food. In the event of equipment breakdown regard must be given to the time period elapsed before discovery of the breakdown.	It is advisable to keep periods where relevant food is out of refrigeration to the minimum possible. Where extensive handling or processing of foods takes place, during which food warms to ambient temperature, consideration should be given to chilling during the process or the use of air-conditioning of the room. It is not advisable to subject a relevant food to more than one period where temperature rises to over 8°C with cooling after.

Provisions Applicable to England, Wales and Northern Ireland

Legal requirement	Guide to compliance	Advice on good practice
temperature control Regulation 8 *No person shall in the course of the activities of a food business keep any food which -* *(a) has been cooked or re-heated;* *(b) is for service or on display for sale; and* *(c) needs to be kept hot in order to control the growth of pathogenic micro-organisms or the formation of toxins, at or in food premises at a temperature below 63°C*	Relevant hot food must be kept at 63°C or more after cooking or reheating, except as described below. Care must be taken to ensure equipment used to keep food hot is capable of maintaining food at 63°C or more.	Hot food should be heated through the 'danger zone' shown on Page 14 quickly. Hot food cabinets are not generally suitable for cooking/heating food. Do not overload cabinets. It is good practice to ensure all food that is re-heated reaches a core temperature of at least 70°C and is held at this for at least 2 minutes.
temperature control Regulation 9 (1) *In any proceedings for an offence of contravening regulation 8, it shall be a defence for a person charged to prove that-* *(a) a well-founded scientific assessment of the safety of the food at temperatures below 63°C has concluded that there is no risk to health if, after cooking or reheating, the food is held for service or on display for sale -* *(i) at a holding temperature which is below 63°C, and* *(ii) for a period not exceeding a specified period of time; and* *(b) at the time of the commission of the alleged offence, the food was held in a manner which is justified in the light of that scientific assessment.*	The obligation in Regulation 8 to keep relevant hot food at 63°C or more can be varied to a different temperature and for a specified time if based on a proper scientific assessment which shows there is no risk to health.	Expert advice should be sought before seeking to rely on this provision.

Food Safety (Temperature Control) Regulations 1995 – Guide to compliance by Retailers

Provisions Applicable to England, Wales and Northern Ireland

Legal requirement	Guide to compliance	Advice on good practice
temperature control Regulation 9 (2)		
In any proceedings for an offence of contravening regulation 8, it shall be a defence for a person charged to prove that the food - *(a) had been kept for service or on display for sale for a period of less than two hours; and* *(b) had not previously been kept for service or on display for sale by that person.*	This provision provides an exception to the obligation in Regulation 8 and allows relevant hot food to be kept at less than 63°C for a single period of not more than 2 hours. It is up to the retailer to be able to show that these limitations have been met. At the end of the time period, food must be disposed of unless a retailer is confident it remains wholesome. In this case it must be chilled to 8°C or less and sold/disposed of within a period which does not pose a risk to health.	If a retailer wishes to use this provision, a system should be established to ensure time limits are effectively applied. It is good practice to limit foods kept below 63°C for display and to dispose of any so kept at the end of the two hour period or chill to 8°C or less and dispose of by the end of the trading day.
temperature control Regulation 11		
A food business responsible for cooling any food which must, by virtue of this Part, be kept at a temperature below ambient temperatures shall cool that food as quickly as possible following -	Where relevant food is, as a result of processing, at temperatures in the 'danger zone', it is important that they are cooled quickly to avoid the risk of growth of bacteria. For foods at or around ambient temperatures it is sufficient to place them in a suitable refrigerator/cold cabinet and the use of equipment such as blast chillers will rarely be required.	Foods should be cooled in such a way that they do not remain in the 'danger zone' for more than 4 hours. Generally, display cabinets are not suitable for reducing food from cooking temperatures.
(a) the final heat processing stage; or *(b) if no heat process is applied, the final preparation stage,* *to the temperature at which, by virtue of this Part, it must be kept.*	Hot foods may be allowed to cool in ambient conditions to near ambient temperatures before being placed in a refrigerator/cold cabinet.	When cooling hot foods good air circulation and breaking food down into small quantities will aid cooling.

Legal requirement	Guide to compliance	Advice on good practice
temperature control Regulation 12 *For the purposes of regulations 6 (2) and 9 (1), the presence of a scientific assessment of the safety of any food in a guide to good hygiene practice which has been -* *(a) forwarded by the Secretary of State to the Commission pursuant to article 5.5 of the Directive, unless the Secretary of State has announced that the guide no longer complies with article 3 of the Directive; or* *(b) developed in accordance with article 5.6 and 7 of the Directive and published in accordance with article 5.8 of the Directive,* *shall, until the contrary is proved, be considered sufficient evidence that the scientific assessment in question is well-founded.*	This provides that any scientific assessments which allow foods to be kept above 8°C or below 63°C which are included in a guide of this type shall be presumed to be well founded. This Guide does not include such assessments.	

Provisions Applicable in Scotland

Legal requirement	Guide to compliance	Advice on good practice
temperature control Regulation 16 (1) *Subject to paragraphs (2) and (3), no person shall in the course of the activities of a food business keep any products which are -* *(a) raw materials, ingredients, intermediate products or finished products; and* *(b) likely to support the growth of pathogenic micro-organisms or the formation of toxins, at temperatures which would result in a risk to health.*	The general obligation to avoid keeping foods at temperatures which would result in a risk to health, as applicable in the rest of the UK, similarly applies in Scotland. The types of food covered by this obligation are the same as those covered by Regulation 10 on Page 15 above and described as 'relevant foods'.	Foods should not be kept in the 'danger zone' described on Page 14 where bacterial growth occurs for any longer than is absolutely necessary.
temperature control Regulation 16 (2) *Consistent with food safety, limited periods outside temperature control are permitted where necessary to accommodate the practicalities of handling during preparation, transport, storage, display and service of food.*	This provision recognises that some variation from usual temperature control is necessary to accommodate handling, preparation etc. Further details on such variation is given below.	

Provisions Applicable in Scotland

Legal requirement	Guide to compliance	Advice on good practice
temperature control Regulation 16 (3) *Paragraph (1) shall not apply to any food which immediately following a final heat processing stage, or a final preparation stage if no heat process is applied, is being cooled as quickly as possible to a temperature which would not result in a risk to health.*	Food which has been heat processed or prepared is not to be treated as in breach of this Regulation if it is immediately after processing or preparation being cooled as quickly as possible to a 'safe' temperature.	Relevant food to be processed or prepared should be kept at ambient temperature for as short a time as possible.
temperature control Regulation 13 (1) *Subject to paragraph (2), no person shall keep food with respect to which any commercial operation is being carried out at or in food premises otherwise than -* *(a) in a refrigerator or refrigerating chamber or in a cool ventilated place; or* *(b) at a temperature above 63 ˚C.*	This builds on the general obligation in Regulation 16 above. Unlike the rest of the UK however, in Scotland no specific temperature is stated. Relevant foods must be kept in a refrigerator/cabinet or a cool ventilated place. Special care must be taken if a refrigerator is not used that the place chosen remains cool when ambient temperatures are high e.g. in Summer. If the place chosen exceeds 8 ˚C then the shelf life of the foodstuff may need to be reduced. Hot foods must be kept at or above 63 ˚C.	It is suggested that all relevant foods should be kept in a refrigerator/cabinet, able to maintain the food at 8 ˚C or less. A cool place should not exceed 10 ˚C.

Legal requirement	Guide to compliance	Advice on good practice
temperature control Regulation 13 (2) *Paragraph (1) shall not apply to any food -* *(a) which is undergoing preparation for sale;* *(b) which is exposed for sale or has been sold to a consumer whether for immediate consumption or otherwise;* *(c) which, immediately following any process of cooking to which it is subjected or the final processing stage if no cooking process is applied, is being cooled under hygienic conditions as quickly as possible to a temperature which would not result in a risk to health;* *(d) which, in order that it may be conveniently available for sale on the premises to consumers, it is reasonable to keep otherwise than as referred to in paragraph (1);* *(e) which, for the duration of its shelf life, may be kept at ambient temperatures with no risk to health;* *(f) to which Council Regulation (EEC) No 1906/90 on certain marketing standards for poultry, as amended, applies;* *(g) to which Council Regulation (EEC) No.1907/90 on certain marketing standards for eggs, as amended, applies.*	The requirement to keep food cool or above 63°C does not apply whilst it is being prepared for sale, on display or is being cooled quickly after processing or preparation. Neither does it apply to product kept for sale where it is not reasonably practicable to keep cool or hot as the case may be. Some foods may have their shelf lives determined so that - though relevant foods - they can be kept at ambient temperature without risk to health. These foods are described in guidance to Regulation 5 (b) above. The guidance given to Regulation 5 (f) and 5 (g) applies here.	Relevant foods should be kept at ambient temperature for the shortest time possible. The quantities of food being prepared or held as back-up stock for service counters, for example should be kept as small as is strictly necessary.

Provisions Applicable in Scotland

Legal requirement	Guide to compliance	Advice on good practice
temperature control Regulation 14 (1) *Food which in the course of a commercial operation has been heated and which is thereafter reheated before being served for immediate consumption or exposed for sale shall, on being reheated, be raised to a temperature of not less than 82 °C.*	Foods which are reheated must be raised to a temperature of not less than 82°C before being displayed/served. This does not apply to foods cooked elsewhere e.g. sausage rolls served hot, but originally baked off the premises. Neither does it apply to foods such as buns or scones to be served warm or toasted. There is no equivalent requirement in the rest of the U.K. Once food exceeds 82°C it may then be kept at over 63°C. The whole of this food must reach 82°C and care must be taken that the temperature and time of heating are sufficient to do this, or the core temperature must be verified by probing.	Food should not be reheated more than once.
temperature control Regulation 14 (2) *In any proceedings for an offence under paragraph (1), it shall be a defence for the person charged to prove that he could not have raised the food to a temperature of not less than 82 °C without a deterioration of its qualities.*	The 82°C re-heating temperature need not be achieved if to do so would cause the food to deteriorate.	It is good practice to ensure all food that is re-heated reaches a core temperature of at least 70°C and is held at this for at least 2 minutes.

Provisions Applicable in Scotland

Legal requirement	Guide to compliance	Advice on good practice
temperature control Regulation 15 (1) and (2) *(1) Gelatine intended for use in the preparation of bakers' confectionery filling, meat products or fish products in the course of the activities of a food business shall, immediately before use, be brought to the boil or brought to and kept at a temperature of not less than 71 °C for 30 minutes.* *(2) Any gelatine left over after the completion of the process shall, if not treated as waste, be cooled under hygienic conditions as quickly as is reasonably practicable and when cold shall be kept in a refrigerator or a refrigerating chamber or a cool ventilated place.*	This is another special requirement for Scotland. Left over gelatine, if not disposed of must be cooled quickly (e.g. sitting pan in cold water) and then kept cool. It must be boiled or kept at 71 °C for 30 minutes again if re-used.	Only sufficient product for immediate needs should be prepared. Any left over product should be disposed of.

Temperature Monitoring

Legal requirement	Guide to compliance	Advice on good practice
	Throughout this section there are references to the need to achieve certain temperatures for relevant foods.	
	In order to ensure that this is done, some monitoring of temperatures in refrigeration cabinets, stores or (in Scotland) ambient conditions must be conducted.	
	Guidance on equipment that can be used and methods of measurement is provided in Appendix II.	
	Each food business must determine the extent of monitoring conducted in the light of methods/equipment used, type of foods sold and product shelf lives.	
	All businesses must conduct a regular check on each refrigeration cabinet or cold store (or hot holding cabinet) to ensure it is working properly.	
	Each cabinet etc. must then be checked on every trading day to verify proper temperatures are maintained.	
	This check must be either -	
	(i) of a built-in thermometer where fitted, provided the equipment producer has not indicated it is unsuitable for this purpose; or	
	(ii) of the air temperature in the cabinet at various places provided the results can be correlated to average cabinet temperature;	
	(iii) of the product using the between-pack method described in Appendix II, or by direct product testing.	
	The Regulations do not require that records are kept of temperature monitoring.	It is good practice to keep some records of temperature checks - See Section 4.11.

Use of Refrigeration Equipment

Refrigerators and display cabinets are designed to hold temperatures at a particular level and not to cool product down.

Legal requirement	Guide to compliance	Advice on good practice
Chapter I 2 *Food Safety (General Food Hygiene) Regulations* *The layout, design, construction and size of food premises shall - (d) provide, where necessary, suitable temperature conditions for the hygienic processing and storage of products.*	Sufficient cabinets/stores must be provided to allow products subject to temperature control to be stored without overloading. In Scotland foods may be kept instead in cool, ventilated places.	Products should be placed in a cabinet/store so as to allow good air circulation and load lines should be observed. Manufacturer's instructions on the siting, use and maintenance of refrigeration equipment should be followed. The siting of cabinets next to doors or by heaters may adversely affect their performance and should be avoided. Doors of refrigerators or stores should be closed when not in use.

TEMPERATURE CONTROL CHECK LIST

This check list has been prepared to help you to judge whether you are complying with the requirements of this section. Whilst it is recommended that you complete it as shown, you are not obliged to do so under the Regulations.

		YES	NO	COMMENTS
1.	Are relevant foods kept at temperatures which do not pose a risk to health?	☐	☐	
2.	Are relevant foods kept at or below 8°C, except where specifically allowed? (Except Scotland)	☐	☐	
3.	Where time periods at ambient are used, is a satisfactory method employed to ensure they are observed?	☐	☐	
4.	In Scotland are relevant foods kept refrigerated or in a cool ventilated place?	☐	☐	
5.	Are relevant hot foods kept at or above 63°C, except where specifically allowed?	☐	☐	
6.	Is refrigeration equipment in good working order?	☐	☐	
7.	Are daily checks conducted to verify temperature controls are being observed?	☐	☐	
8.	In Scotland, are reheated foods raised to 82°C prior to display or sale?	☐	☐	
9.	In Scotland, are the requirements for gelatine being observed?	☐	☐	
10.	When heating or cooling foods are they taken through the 'danger zone' quickly?	☐	☐	

Some of the questions may not be applicable to your particular business and you can, if you wish, note this in the comments.

If the answer to all questions is Yes (or not applicable) then the requirements of this section will have been met. If any questions are answered No, comments should be written alongside and improvements necessary should be entered on the assessment chart.

PRODUCT HANDLING

Introduction

Good product handling is an essential element in the control of each of the three major hazards. Great care must be taken during all stages of the handling that the food undergoes, i.e. delivery, storage, preparation, display and sale to ensure that they have been carried out as hygienically as possible.

Legal requirement	Guide to compliance	Advice on good practice
Chapter IX 1		
No raw materials or ingredients shall be accepted by a food business if they are known to be, or might reasonably be expected to be, so contaminated with parasites, pathogenic micro-organisms, or toxic, decomposed or foreign substances, that after normal sorting and/or preparatory or processing procedures hygienically applied by food businesses, they would still be unfit for human consumption.	Any retail operation must have an effective receiving system to ensure the safety of food delivered. It is recommended that deliveries are checked for signs of visible damage or contamination and for date codes.	All deliveries should be checked against the description, order and delivery note.
	Verify chilled and frozen foods are suitably cold on delivery.	Reading of a temperature measuring device on the delivery vehicle or the use of a thermometer to check temperature is good practice.
	Any deliveries showing signs of infestation, damage or soiling must be rejected.	It is recommended that a responsible and designated person is assigned to receive the deliveries. This person should have sufficient knowledge to ensure products are properly received.
		Copies of the delivery notes and details of any rejected products should be kept.
		Record temperature checks.

Storage

Legal requirement	Guide to Compliance	Advice on good practice
Chapter IX 2 *Raw materials and ingredients stored in the establishment shall be kept in appropriate conditions designed to prevent harmful deterioration and to protect them from contamination.*	Foods must be kept in storage conditions which are appropriate to the nature of the product. Dry goods must be stored in an area that is clean, dry and infestation free. Fruit and vegetables must be stored in a clean, infestation free area. Chilled foods must be placed without delay into clean chilled storage. Frozen food must be placed as soon as practicable into freezer storage.	After a delivery has been accepted, the food should be taken immediately to a designated storage area. Dry goods should be stored off the floor. Extremes of temperature and humidity should be avoided in store rooms. Raw meat and fish should be kept in chilled storage. Food which has defrosted should not be refrozen without obtaining expert advice.

Protection from contamination

Contamination may be either physical or bacterial.

Generally bacterial contamination is likely to render foods either unfit, e.g. putrid, or injurious to health, e.g. containing bacterial toxins. A special type of contamination is cross-contamination by bacteria from one material to another. This is explained below.

Physical contamination with foreign objects or chemicals will usually result in it being unreasonable to expect the food to be consumed in that state.

In addition, physical damage to foods or their containers can result in contamination. If cans or vacuum packs become punctured the food inside will rapidly deteriorate.

Legal requirement	Guide to Compliance	Advice on good practice
Chapter IX 3 *All food which is handled, stored, packaged, displayed and transported, shall be protected against any contamination likely to render the food unfit for human consumption, injurious to health or contaminated in such a way that it would be unreasonable to expect it to be consumed in that state. In particular, food must be so placed and / or protected as to minimise any risk of contamination.*	Avoidance of contamination requires constant attention but methods employed will vary depending on the nature of the product. High risk, open foods are particularly susceptible and special care must be taken with these. Such foods must be physically protected e.g. by placing them in containers, covering them and/or by placing them where foreign objects can not drop on to them. Raw and cooked foods must be stored apart or covered with suitable wrappings. Separate utensils must if possible be used for raw and cooked foods. Where separate equipment such as slicers cannot be provided, it must be thoroughly washed and disinfected between use on raw and cooked foods.	Open foods or foods not in impervious packing should not be placed on the floor. Physical dividers should be used between raw and cooked foods in any shared display cabinet. Raw meat, fish and poultry should be kept in containers to avoid spillage of juices etc. and must be placed below ready to eat foods in refrigerators or in Scotland a larder. Separate refrigerators for raw and cooked foods should be used. The use of colour coded knives, chopping boards etc. should be used. Separate equipment for raw and cooked foods is recommended.
Chapter IX 4 *Hazardous and/or inedible substances, including animal feedstuffs, shall be adequately labelled and stored in separate and secure containers.*	Hazardous materials such as cleaning chemicals or lubricants must be stored away from food to avoid accidental contamination or taint. Containers must be clearly labelled. Do not use food containers to store hazardous materials.	Containers should be sealed. If original packaging is not used, any new containers should be properly labelled with the contents and safety/usage instructions.

BACKGROUND INFORMATION

Cross Contamination

Bacteria cannot move by themselves but are transferred from the source of the bacteria to foods either directly or indirectly.

Directly, requires the source of the bacteria to be in actual contact with the food. An example of direct contamination is when cooked meats are touching raw sausage or other meat whilst on display because there is not a physical divider between them. Another example is when raw meat is stored above ready to eat food, in a refrigerator. Juices from the raw meat containing food poisoning bacteria could accidentally drip onto the food stored below.

Indirectly, relies on an intermediary or vehicle to transfer the bacteria. The following items may be considered as possible vehicles of indirect cross contamination: slicers, knives, tongs, cutting boards, cleaning cloths, scales, spoons, hands, trays, preparation surfaces and insects. If any of these items come into contact with raw foods and then come into contact with ready to eat foods then they have become vehicles of cross contamination for the bacteria.

An example of how bacteria may be transferred indirectly is as follows:

Raw product handled - Hands wiped on cloth - Knife wiped with cloth - Knife used to cut cooked meat.

PRODUCT HANDLING CHECK LIST

This check list has been prepared to help you to judge whether you are complying with the requirements of this section. Whilst it is recommended that you complete it as shown, you are not obliged to do so under the Regulations.

		YES	NO	COMMENTS
1.	Are deliveries checked on receipt, including verification that chilled and frozen foods are suitably cold?	☐	☐	
2.	Are chilled and frozen foods transferred as required from delivery to coldstore or display?	☐	☐	
3.	Are all open high risk foods covered or protected whilst in storage or on display?	☐	☐	
4.	Are open raw and cooked foods physically separated at all times?	☐	☐	
5.	Do you use separate utensils for raw and cooked foods?	☐	☐	
6.	If separate equipment is not available is it washed and disinfected between being used for raw and cooked foods?	☐	☐	
7.	Are dry goods stored in a clean dry area?	☐	☐	
8.	Do you ensure foods are not stored with non-foods that may taint or contaminate them?	☐	☐	

Some questions may not be applicable to your particular business and you can if you wish note this in the comments.

If the answer to all questions is Yes (or not applicable) then the requirements of this section will have been met. If any questions are answered No, comments should be written alongside and improvements necessary should be entered on the assessment chart.

STOCK ROTATION

Introduction

The correct storage and stock rotation of food is fundamental to the hygienic and profitable operation of any food business. Failure to ensure such good practices can result in problems of unfit or spoiled food and also considerable reduction in the shelf life of products.

Food Labelling Legislation requires that the shelf life of most foods be clearly indicated. This has to be either a "Best Before" or for highly microbiologically perishable foods a "Use By" date. It is an offence to sell food after its use by date.

Stock rotation applies to all food types and failure to rotate stock can allow the product to become unmarketable due to staleness or changes in texture or colour. More serious problems may be caused by mould growth, infestations by insects, rancidity, slime and off odours. Stock which is left undisturbed for any period will encourage infestations.

Stock rotation is particularly important for high risk foods where microbiological growth can readily occur.

Legal requirement	Guide to compliance	Advice on good practice
Chapter IX 3 *All food which is handled, stored, packaged, displayed and transported, shall be protected against any contamination likely to render the food unfit for human consumption, injurious to health or contaminated in such a way that it would be unreasonable to expect it to be consumed in that state.*	Most foodstuffs are marked with an indication of the period for which they are expected to remain safe and wholesome when kept in specified conditions. For high risk foods the shelf life is a major factor in controlling the safety of the product and avoiding the hazard of microbiological growth which could, over time, render the food unfit or injurious to health. Control of shelf life (stock rotation) is therefore an important protection against contamination. When stock deliveries arrive sample date codes must be checked to ensure that product received is in code and has sufficient life to enable it to be sold within its life. This is particularly important for products marked with a "use by" date. For loose products such as meat or items displayed on a delicatessen counter, products that do not carry a date code, and those manufactured in store or which are exempt from marking, a system is required to ensure products are rotated on a "first in, first out" basis. Once outer casings/wrappings have been removed and products opened, their original code life may be shortened.	For unmarked foods it is recommended that dates of arrival / production are marked on boxes or individual ticketing and the period of display also marked. Alternative methods such as the use of coloured stickers or product books can also be used provided the system is understood by staff. It is advised you seek this information from your supplier to ensure products are not stored beyond an appropriate fitness date. Record date of opening.

Legal requirement	Guide to compliance	Advice on good practice
Chapter IX 3	Product must be stored in the necessary conditions applicable, i.e. freezer, refrigerator or dry store.	Old stock should be pulled to the front and the new stock stored at the rear.
	Effective and regular code checks must be carried out on short life perishable foods on display. This would apply to all high risk foods and also short life products such as bread and fresh meat or fish. This is most effectively done at replenishment.	When replenishing short life products into chilled cabinets or display shelves it is good practice to rotate all the display to place older stock at the front and fill up from the back. In this way any products nearing the end of their life will be brought to notice.
	Longer life "best before" foods must be checked at a frequency determined by the length of product life and turnover of products. This will be less frequent than that of "use by" coded products.	"Best before" coded items with a life of 1 - 3 months, or less, should be checked monthly.
	Long life foods (18 months or more) must be checked according to turnover of product. If good stock rotation is adhered to when products are displayed this should highlight any products nearing the end of their life.	Any very slow moving products should be checked at six monthly intervals. It may be useful to incorporate code checking of longer life products such as tinned and dried products into a shelf cleaning programme. As displays are cleared for cleaning, codes can be checked and stock rotated as required.
	Any foods marked with a "use by" date indication that exceed their code life must be removed from sale and transferred to an identified place where customers do not have access whilst awaiting disposal, so as to ensure that such food does not re-enter the food chain.	Foods marked with a "best before" or "best before end" code should be removed from sale when their code life has expired.

BACKGROUND INFORMATION

Date Coding

The form of date marking used depends upon the expected life of the product. This is set out in the Food Labelling Regulations 1996 and summarised below.

Expected Shelf Life	Date Marking Allowable
Highly perishable and likely to constitute an immediate danger to health (short life products).	USE BY .... Day........... Month ...... or .... Day........... Month . ....Year
3 months or less	BEST BEFORE .... Day .... Month ...... or Day.......... Month .....Year
3 to 18 months	BEST BEFORE .... Day .... Month .....Year or BEST BEFORE END .... Month .....Year
More than 18 months	BEST BEFORE .... Day.......... Month ......Year or BEST BEFORE END .... Month ......Year or BEST BEFORE END ....Year

NB: It is an offence to alter or remove a "use by" date mark if you are not yourself the person who originally applied the date mark, or do not have their written permission to make such a change.

The following foods are exempt from date marking:

Fresh fruit and vegetables which have not been peeled or cut into pieces. This includes potatoes but not sprouting seeds, legumes, bean sprouts or similar products;

Wine, alcoholic drinks (10% or more alcoholic strength);

Soft drinks (greater than 5 litres for catering premises);

Vinegar, salt, sugar, chewing gum;

Flour confectionery and bread if it is intended to be consumed within 24 hours of preparation;

Edible ices in individual portions;

Those foods prepared on the retail premises for direct sale.

STOCK ROTATION CHECK LIST

This check list has been prepared to help you to judge whether you are complying with the requirements of this section. Whilst it is recommended that you complete it as shown, you are not obliged to do so under the Regulations.

		YES	NO	COMMENTS
1.	Are sample product date codes checked on delivery?	☐	☐	
2.	Are products stored so as to assist 'first in, first out' rotation?	☐	☐	
3.	Do you carry out regular checks on short life foods?	☐	☐	
4.	Do you carry out checks on longer life foods as recommended?	☐	☐	
5.	For foods sold from loose, produced in store or which are exempt from date marking, is a system used to determine product life?	☐	☐	
6.	Are staff familiar with date code checking and monitoring?	☐	☐	
7.	Are out of date foods to be disposed of kept separate in a place where customers do not have access?	☐	☐	

Some questions may not be applicable to your particular business and you can if you wish note this in the comments.

If the answer to all questions is Yes (or not applicable) then the requirements of this section will have been met. If any questions are answered No, comments should be written alongside and improvements necessary should be entered on the assessment chart.

Introduction

Cleaning is essential to control the hazards of microbiological and physical contamination of foods in the retail environment. Different standards will be applicable for store rooms for packaged foods and for areas where high risk open food is being prepared, but generally cleanliness of equipment and structure throughout the premises is important in order to convey a positive image to customers and staff and a safe and efficient working environment.

The effectiveness of cleaning will depend upon the frequency (how often you clean) and the methods used.

Legal requirement	Guide to compliance	Advice on good practice
Chapter I 1 *Food premises must be kept clean and maintained in good repair and condition.*	The degree of cleanliness required depends both upon the use of the premises and also the nature of the food being dealt with. Reception areas, store rooms, chillers and other parts of the premises where open food is not kept, must be free from accumulated dirt and debris that may, for example, encourage pests. Floors must be regularly swept/ vacuumed or washed as appropriate. In food preparation areas or at service counters, surfaces which may come into contact with food must be visibly clean of dirt, grease and food debris before work commences. Other parts of the preparation area such as high wall surfaces and ventilation ducts must be cleaned periodically such that dirt is not allowed to accumulate to levels where contamination of food may occur.	Regular cleaning throughout the working period (clean as you go) is good practice and prevents build up of dirt. In food preparation areas, spillages should be dealt with as they occur. The use of compounds to absorb spills is acceptable provided they are removed when this is achieved and care is taken to protect any open foods from contamination. Preventative spreading of absorbents is not good practice.
Chapter V 1 *All articles, fittings and equipment with which food comes into contact shall be kept clean*	Food contact surfaces, equipment etc. must be kept clean and be thoroughly cleaned at the end of each shift or day. In addition to cleaning, open food contact surfaces, equipment and utensils must be disinfected periodically to prevent build up of unseen bacteria. Proprietors of businesses must ensure that the type and frequency of cleaning of the premises, equipment etc. is understood and followed. Written cleaning schedules are not mandatory.	Items which are regularly handled such as refrigerator, drawer or door handles should also be periodically disinfected. Cleaning schedules will be of assistance, particularly in larger premises and can incorporate a record to show work required has been done

BACKGROUND INFORMATION

Effective Cleaning

For cleaning to be effective, hot water, a detergent and some physical effort is needed. A detergent is a chemical which helps to dissolve grease and remove dirt.

Even if a surface looks clean, it may still have bacteria on it. Where it is necessary to make sure that it is safe it should be disinfected. Disinfection is the reduction of bacteria to a safe level. The most common way to disinfect is to use very hot water or a suitable chemical disinfectant.

The application of heat is the most reliable and effective means of destroying bacteria although this may not always be the most practical. Temperatures in dishwashers and sterilising sinks, where articles are fully immersed for approximately 30 seconds reach over 80°C and this will effectively disinfect. Don't then dry with "dirty" towels!

Another chemical which facilitates effective cleaning is a **sanitizer**. This is a chemical which incorporates both a detergent and a disinfectant so is able to clean, by dissolving grease and dirt, and disinfect, by reducing bacteria to a safe level. This chemical combines two stages of cleaning but do not try to combine two chemicals into one yourself. Sanitizers are produced by all of the leading chemical manufacturers.

It is important that any cleaning operation does not in itself cause further problems. If not removed themselves, cleaning or disinfecting solutions and cleaning equipment can contaminate foods. Any open foods in the vicinity of the area to be cleaned should be removed or if this is not practicable, securely covered with impervious material.

What to Disinfect?

The simple rule to remember is that: all food contact and hand contact surfaces can be covered in bacteria which need to be restricted to a safe level to avoid food poisoning, food spoilage and cross-contamination.

As bacteria are not mobile and need to be physically carried onto food, the disinfection of non-food contact surfaces such as floors and walls, is rarely needed and a detergent would suffice.

Disinfection, or alternatively the use of a sanitizer should normally therefore be restricted to:

- all direct food contact surfaces, including work tops and equipment;
- hand contact surfaces such as doors;
- cleaning materials and equipment including cloths, bowls and brushes.

Disinfection Frequency

In most operations contamination by bacteria takes time to build up to a significant level and under normal circumstances therefore disinfection can correspond with cleaning intervals dictated by visual soiling or work cycles. However, additional disinfection will be needed in practices involving the production and handling of high risk foods, ie. delicatessen counters and also where raw foods, such as raw meats could contaminate work surfaces and equipment and so cross contaminate cooked products, e.g., butchery areas.

Frequency of Cleaning

The effectiveness of cleaning will depend upon the frequency and the methods used. "Clean as you go" is a policy that will help ensure that things do not become so dirty during the working day that thorough cleaning ultimately becomes very difficult and labour intensive. Clean as you go involves keeping work surfaces and areas uncluttered, frequently removing waste and rubbish, together with any unwanted tools or equipment.

It also involves the regular wiping down with a disinfectant (or sanitizer) to restrict bacteria to a safe level in all work areas before, during and after food preparation/handling takes place.

This approach to cleaning is best practice and other methods that achieve the required standard of cleanliness are acceptable.

BACKGROUND INFORMATION

Examples of 'clean as you go'

- **Butchery:** Scraping off all meat and blood residues from the preparation table and wiping over with sanitizing solution prior to taking a break or changing the type of work being done - so that the table is clean prior to re-commencing work.

- **Bakery:** Brushing off all loose flour and debris from baking trays after use - prior to returning trays to the production area so that the spare trays are always clean and no dirty trays are being stored in the bakery.

- **Delicatessen/Provisions:** Wiping down the food slicer with a clean sanitized cloth after use to remove all loose meat and food residues - even if there is no time to thoroughly strip and clean the machine - this can be carried out later when time permits.

- **Close of trading:** At the end of production, or at the end of the trading day 'Close of trading cleaning' should take place - all food and hand contact surfaces should be disinfected or sanitized.

How to Clean

There can be as many as six stages in achieving the desired level of cleanliness - very often failure to clean involves a failure to carry out one or more of these stages - resulting in smear marks or food debris remaining on the surface of equipment or bacteria being allowed to survive.

The six stages of cleaning:

1.	Pre-clean	Scrape or wipe off loose dirt or waste food.
2.	Main Clean	Wash or scrub with detergent in hot water, changing when dirty, to remove all grease and waste food/dirt.
3.	Rinse	To remove detergent and dissolved dirt.
4.	Disinfect	A second wash with a food-safe disinfectant to reduce to safe levels any bacteria which may remain.
5.	Final Rinse	To remove any traces of disinfectant.
6.	Dry/buff	Air drying or use of clean disposable cloth or paper towels.

The use of a "sanitizer" can reduce the cleaning procedure by combining 2 to 4. A "non-rinse" residual surface sanitizer will reduce the stages further still, allowing for surfaces to be cleaned and bacteria killed.

Not all stages will be required in every case. It has already been said that some surfaces will not need disinfecting for example, and step 1 could be omitted if soiling was not significant. Two examples are shown below which illustrate the use of these stages.

Preparation Table

- Scrape off or wipe off all loose debris (French scraper). (Step 1 Pre-clean)

- Clean with a sanitizer solution. Use a scouring pad or brush to work loose any stubborn stains. (Steps 2 to 4)

- Rinse using clean, hot water to remove loosened dirt. (Step 5)

- Wipe off excess water with a clean disposable cloth and allow to air dry. (Step 6)

- Do not forget to clean underneath the table and to clean the frame.

BACKGROUND INFORMATION

Small Equipment - eg. Provisions Trays

- Scrape/wipe off all loose debris. (Step 1)

- Wash using detergent solution. Use a pad or brush to work in detergent to all areas and to loosen grease deposits. (Step 2)

- Rinse in clean hot water. (Step 3)

- Wash with disinfectant solution. (Step 4)

- Rinse in clean hot water. (Step 5)

- Air dry on draining area. (Step 6)

Chemical Control

To avoid confusion the number of different cleaning chemicals available for use should be minimised.

Chemicals should be stored in original containers and used before the expiry date. In no circumstances should chemicals be placed in unmarked containers. Care must be taken when making up cleaning solutions and manufacturers' instructions must always be followed. The Employer has a responsibility under the *Control of Substances Hazardous to Health Regulations* to ensure the safety of employees whilst handling chemicals. In the case of an accident involving chemicals follow manufacturers' recommendations.

Choosing Your Cleaning Chemicals

When choosing chemicals for use, consider the following:

- The possibility of taint to food products - specialist food grade chemicals are recommended.

- Toxicity of the chemical and its possible effect on personnel. The necessary protective equipment such as gloves, goggles or face masks must be provided as recommended by the manufacturers' instruction. Your staff will need to be aware of the safe use of chemicals.

- The type of disinfectant needed may vary according to the type of soiling, type of bacteria, contact time available and type of surface to be cleaned. It is recommended that advice is sought from professional cleaning companies or material suppliers if you are in doubt.

Equipment

It should be ensured that cleaning equipment itself is kept clean and in a condition of good repair and replaced as necessary when worn or defective. Equipment should be stored in a designated area.

A vast range of specialist equipment is available for cleaning operations and the correct choice for your business will ensure effective cleaning is carried out.

Cleaning Cloths

These vary from the durable, high strength textile cloths to the semi-disposable, non-woven absorbent variety. Disposable paper is commonly used in preference to cloths. Cloths can carry bacteria so it is essential that they are clean and regularly changed. Unclean cloths will spread contamination from one area to another and therefore it is best to start with lightly soiled areas. Remember, "a cloth is only as clean as the last thing it was used on!" Cloths should be free of loose threads which could contaminate food or equipment.

BACKGROUND INFORMATION

Where both raw and cooked foods are handled separate cleaning cloths should be used. Different colour clothes for different areas will assist. If not disposable, cloths should be washed regularly and allowed to air-dry.

Brushes

Plastic brushes are preferable to wood and bristle brushes as they are capable of withstanding boiling water and chemical solutions and the security of the fibres is generally much better.

Mops and Buckets

Mops should be thoroughly cleaned after use and buckets emptied and then left to air dry. Do not store mops in buckets, since drying is impaired.

Mechanical Aids

These include floor cleaning machines, power washers, steam cleaners, vacuum pick-ups and dishwashing machines. Judicious use can reduce labour requirements but care should be taken to ensure that any piece of equipment is suitable for the use intended and is properly maintained.

The Use of Contractors

It is often worth considering the use of specialist cleaning contractors to supplement your own cleaning for intensive deep cleaning of the structure, ventilation trunking, drains and difficult to reach surfaces. For larger premises contractors can also conduct routine cleaning at the end of the day's trading, though the use of contractors is not a substitute for 'cleaning as you go' throughout the day. Where contractors are used, the retailer still retains the responsibility for ensuring compliance with the Regulations.

CLEANING CHECK LIST

This check list has been prepared to help you to judge whether you are complying with the requirements of this section. Whilst it is recommended that you complete it as shown, you are not obliged to do so under the Regulations.

		YES	NO	COMMENTS
1.	Have I devised suitable cleaning arrangements for all areas of my food business?	☐	☐	
2.	Are standards of cleanliness monitored to ensure that effective cleaning is being carried out?	☐	☐	
3.	Are correct cleaning methods and materials being used for the appropriate areas?	☐	☐	
4.	Are high wall surfaces, ceilings, ventilation ducts etc. periodically cleaned?	☐	☐	
5.	Is the proper usage of cleaning chemicals provided for, ie. storage, use of protective equipment, adherence to manufacturers' recommendations and staff awareness?	☐	☐	
6.	Is equipment provided for cleaning suitable for its intended use, kept clean and in good condition?	☐	☐	

Some questions may not be applicable to your particular business and you can if you wish note this in the comments .

If the answer to all questions is Yes (or not applicable) then the requirements of this section will have been met. If any questions are answered No, comments should be written alongside and improvements necessary should be entered on the assessment chart.

Introduction

A high standard of personal hygiene is essential in a food business, especially where any open foods are involved. Many potential contaminants of food come directly from the person handling that food e.g. hair, fibres, buttons etc or alternatively, the handler can act as a means of transferring bacteria from their bodies or some other source onto foods. Staff with bad habits will not only distress the customer but could also cause physical harm, or illness due to food poisoning.

Legal requirement	Guide to compliance	Advice on good practice
Chapter VIII 1 *Every person working in a food handling area shall maintain a high degree of personal cleanliness*	Whilst it is desirable that all staff in retail premises display good personal hygiene, those who only work in an office, or a warehouse - driving a fork lift truck for example, and do not come directly into contact with food are not covered by this requirement. It does apply to all staff who work - even occasionally - in food handling areas. Staff involved with replenishing shop floor displays and on checkouts in self-service stores should be treated as food handlers. Particular importance must be given to staff who prepare or handle open food. Open food handlers must wash hands at the start of work and regularly throughout the day. This is particularly important after visiting the lavatory, cleaning, handling food waste or outer packaging (e.g. boxes) and especially between touching raw and cooked foods or their equipment and utensils. Other food handlers must keep hands clean by washing in running water with soap or proprietary cleanser. Hands should be washed at the start of work, after breaks or visiting the lavatory or handling refuse. Where food handlers receive cuts or grazes, they must ensure the wound is fully covered with a purpose-made waterproof dressing. Nail varnish, false nails and perfumed hand cream must not be used if handling open food.	Where frequent hand-washing is required the use of a special food-safe barrier cream may be beneficial. It is good practice to use a bactericidal detergent or wipes where high risk open foods are being handled. Where gloves or other barrier handling techniques are used the same rules for hand-cleaning should still apply. Gloves should be regularly changed as they become soiled or damaged. Dressings should be brightly coloured (usually blue) to be readily visible if displaced. All food handlers should avoid wearing nail varnish, false nails or perfumed hand cream. The use of strong perfumes/after shaves should be avoided where open food such as meats or dairy products which can absorb smells are being handled and could become tainted.

Legal requirement	Guide to compliance	Advice on good practice
	Hair may directly contaminate food and be a source of bacteria if touched. Open high risk food handlers must therefore keep hair clean, with long hair tied back.	For staff preparing food, hats which effectively cover the hair should be worn. Hair nets or snoods may be used in place of or in addition to hats.
	Jewellery - This can both harbour dirt and bacteria and itself contaminate food as a foreign object.	
	Open high risk food handlers should not wear watches, ornate rings, bangles, necklaces etc. Plain band rings and sleeper type earrings only are acceptable.	Sleeper type earrings should be one piece only.
	Smoking or spitting in food handling areas is strictly prohibited. Staff must not eat or drink whilst handling food.	
	Food handlers must not behave in a way that may spread bacteria, e.g. by biting nails, licking fingers, blowing into bags or coughing and sneezing over open food.	
Chapter VIII 1 *and shall wear suitable, clean and, where appropriate, protective clothing.*	Clothing is a common source of contamination of food. Buttons, fibres and debris may fall into food and clothing which is dirty may cause cross-contamination. Ordinary domestic clothing is seldom designed so as to be suitable for open food handling and may easily become soiled.	
	In all cases food handlers must wear clothing that is clean, reasonably fitting and have no loose buttons etc.	Protective clothing should generally be light coloured and have as few pockets as necessary.
	Where open high risk foods are being handled protective clothing <u>must</u> be worn. This would ordinarily include a coat, jacket or similar garment which would cover the arms and body to below waist level. In some areas such as bakeries purpose made protective clothing has been developed and the use of this is acceptable. It must be changed regularly depending on the degree of soiling.	All other open food handlers should wear some protective clothing such as an apron, tabard or coat. Special protective clothing such as sleeve covers, insulated jackets etc. should be provided if required. Staff who handle open high risk foods should not travel to and from work in protective clothing, except where changing facilities are unavailable and in which case final overwear such as an apron should be provided.

Legal requirement	Guide to compliance	Advice on good practice

Chapter VIII 2

No person, known or suspected to be suffering from, or to be a carrier of, a disease likely to be transmitted through food or while afflicted, for example with infected wounds, skin infections, sores or with diarrhoea, shall be permitted to work in any food handling area in any capacity in which there is any likelihood of directly or indirectly contaminating food with pathogenic micro-organisms.

Regulation 5 (1)

Proprietors of food businesses have a duty to exclude members of staff from activities where, because of one of the conditions listed in the Regulation, there may be a risk of staff contaminating food. If, however, warehousemen handle only cans of food there is no reason why they cannot continue - provided they do not come into contact with other higher risk food handlers.

A proprietor must ensure staff are aware of the obligation they are under to report any illness mentioned, or other illness such as vomiting which could be food related.

New food handling staff should be asked whether they have any history of the relevant illnesses and if in doubt a medical report should be obtained before commencing work.

Further information on staff health can be found in the document 'Food Handlers Fitness to Work' from the Department of Health. A copy of this document should be obtained and read.

Subject to paragraph (2), a person working in a food handling area who -
(a) knows or suspects that he is suffering from or that he is a carrier of a disease likely to be transmitted through food; or
(b) is afflicted with an infected wound, a skin infection, sores, diarrhoea or with any analogous medical condition,
in circumstances where there is any likelihood of him directly or indirectly contaminating any food with pathogenic micro-organisms, shall report that knowledge, suspicion or affliction to the proprietor of the food business at which he is working.

Regulation 5 (2)

This requirement applies where a food handler works in a capacity where there is a likelihood they may contaminate food. This must be presumed for anyone handling open foods but other cases must be examined individually.

Where an individual has been excluded from their work on health grounds they should not re-commence their normal duties until they have been symptom free for 48 hours.

Where a food handler has been formally excluded from work by an officer of the local authority or of the health authority (usually a Consultant in Communicable Disease Control), the person must not return to work until notified by the officer that they can do so.

Retailers should include in contracts/particulars of employment a requirement to report illnesses etc. On receiving a report from a member of staff that they may be affected by a disease, illness etc. as described, it is good practice for the proprietor to consult a doctor, occupational health adviser or EHO for advice on whether to exclude the person from their normal work.

Positive clearance by a medical practitioner should be obtained before re-commencing work.

Further information on staff health can be found in the document 'Food Handlers Fitness to Work' from the Department of Health. A copy of this document should be obtained and read.

This regulation shall not apply to a person unless he is working in a food handling area in which a food business proprietor, seeking to comply with regulation 4 (2) (d) and paragraph 2 of Chapter VIII of Schedule 1, may be required to refuse him permission to work.

Guidance to this requirement is included above.

PERSONAL HYGIENE CHECK LIST

This check list has been prepared to help you to judge whether you are complying with the requirements of this section. Whilst it is recommended that you complete it as shown, you are not obliged to do so under the Regulations.

		YES	NO	COMMENTS
1.	Do open food handlers regularly wash their hands?	☐	☐	
2.	Do other food handlers wash hands as required?	☐	☐	
3.	Do open food handlers wear dressings on cuts and grazes?	☐	☐	
4.	Do high risk open food handlers wear hats?	☐	☐	
5.	Is the wearing of jewellery and nail varnish properly controlled?	☐	☐	
6.	Is suitable protective clothing provided if needed?	☐	☐	
7.	Is smoking, eating and drinking by food handlers prohibited whilst working?	☐	☐	
8.	Are staff aware of their responsibility to report diseases/illnesses?	☐	☐	
9.	Are staff who may contaminate food as a result of illness excluded from working in the risk area?	☐	☐	

Some questions may not be applicable to your particular business and you can if you wish note this in the comments.

If the answer to all questions is Yes (or not applicable) then the requirements of this section will have been met. If any questions are answered No, comments should be written alongside and improvements necessary should be entered on the assessment chart.

Introduction

Because open foods are at greater risk of contamination from the environment than wrapped or packaged foods, greater care must be taken when selling them. Good hygiene practices and high standards of cleanliness must be maintained at all times to minimise the risk of food hazards occurring. All open food displays need to be supervised or inspected regularly by staff. Any obvious contamination or damage can in this way be detected and products removed from display if unsuitable for sale.

As outlined in Part II of this guide the most important hazard to foods is that of microbiological contamination. This is a particularly significant hazard when selling open foods from the high or medium risk categories. These foods are likely to support the growth of bacteria if contaminated and stored incorrectly. Contamination of these products can occur readily when displayed in an open way by coming into contact with contaminated containers, equipment and utensils, hands, cleaning cloths or pests.

The hazards of physical contamination and physical damage are likely to occur in all open foods whether high, medium or low risk. As these can lead to serious injury as well as to products not of the required quality, all open foods must be protected as far as possible from these hazards.

Legal requirement	Guide to compliance	Advice on good practice
Chapter IX 3 *All food which is handled, stored, packaged, displayed and transported, shall be protected against any contamination likely to render the food unfit for human consumption, injurious to health or contaminated in such a way that it would be unreasonable to expect it to be consumed in that state. In particular, food must be so placed and/or protected as to minimise any risk of contamination.*	This means all foods must be actively protected from contamination. For foods which require temperature control for their safety, a suitable means of maintaining them at safe temperatures is required. In most cases products will be chilled and must be held at or below 8°C. In Scotland different provisions apply and guidance to these requirements is provided in Section 4.1. Display equipment must be designed and built using suitable materials to give a high standard of food safety. If self service displays such as salad bars are being used there must be effective protection from contamination. The use of a screen, shield or cover that allows access to the product while preventing contamination from above, or the covering of containers for product are among the acceptable ways of achieving this.	Where open high risk foods are made available for customer self selection, particular care should be taken to avoid contamination. All preparation procedures should be carried out quickly and product transferred promptly to the display unit.

Legal requirement	Guide to compliance	Advice on good practice
Chapter IX 3	It is not necessary to provide covers etc. for unwrapped, whole fruits or vegetables.	
	Special care must be taken to avoid cross contamination where both raw and ready to eat foods are being handled.	Designated serving utensils are recommended for particulate or semi-solid products ie. salads, hummus, cream cheese etc. This will prevent physical contamination of one product with another which is clearly undesirable and may be hazardous.
	Physical handling of product should be minimised.	The use of a barrier which prevents hands touching product directly is recommended. Suitable barriers include utensils, film-wrap, paper, reversed food bags or gloves.
	Scrupulous standards of personal hygiene are required when handling and serving high risk open foods. High levels of staff knowledge are required in such service areas to ensure staff are aware of hazards to food and their responsibility to control those hazards.	High risk products displayed openly as samples for customers should be provided in a clean container with a suitable disposable implement available for customer use.
	For self service displays of dry goods regular inspection of product to see if there is contamination or damage is essential. It is recommended that goods such as dried fruits, nuts, cereals or sweets and snacks be displayed in covered display units constructed of hard wearing, readily cleanable material.	
	Open foods must be displayed in such a position as to minimise the risk of contamination. Where foods are positioned outside of premises, for example on a pavement, it is recommended that they should be stored at least 0.5m from the ground and additional precautions taken to avoid other sources of contamination if necessary.	
	For all high risk and medium risk foods it is recommended that a coding system is used for opened and merchandised products that relates to the keeping quality of the products and ensures that foods are sold only within their permitted lives.	

Legal requirement	Guide to compliance	Advice on good practice
Chapter IX 3	Each product must be given a shelf life once opened that will ensure the product is safe when purchased as long as it is stored under the correct conditions. Decisions must be based on technical assessments. Advice may be available from suppliers. Methods for keeping shelf life code with products may include a label displayed with them indicating date by which product must be sold or a code book recording all product on display and date by which it must be sold.	

DISPLAY OF OPEN FOODS CHECK LIST

This check list has been prepared to help you to judge whether you are complying with the requirements of this section. Whilst it is recommended that you complete it as shown, you are not obliged to do so under the Regulations.

		YES	NO	COMMENTS
1.	Are open raw products i.e., fresh meat and poultry segregated from cooked/ready to eat products at all times?	☐	☐	
2.	Is there a system in place for determining shelf life of all open products on display?	☐	☐	
3.	Is staff handling of open high risk products kept to a minimum?	☐	☐	
4.	If high risk self service foods are displayed are they supervised/inspected by a member of staff?	☐	☐	
5.	Are all self service dry goods displayed in suitable containers?	☐	☐	
6.	Are open products such as salad items protected by sneezeguards or suitable barriers to prevent customer tampering?	☐	☐	
7.	Are open food displays routinely inspected to maintain good hygiene standards and appearance of products?	☐	☐	

Some questions may not be applicable to your particular business and you can if you wish note this in the comments .

If the answer to all questions is Yes (or not applicable) then the requirements of this section will have been met. If any questions are answered No, comments should be written alongside and improvements necessary should be entered on the assessment chart.

Introduction

The supervision and instruction and/or training of food handlers is an essential activity in any food business if employees are to understand how they can contribute to food safety and so that they may appreciate how to deal with food hazards.

Not all staff will need the same level of supervision and instruction or training. It will depend upon the work they do and type of foods handled. It is important to note that the Regulations do not require attendance on external training courses. Whilst some of these may be valuable, businesses may choose to provide instruction or training themselves, if suitably skilled staff are available.

This part of the Guide is intended to help you to find the best option for your business.

For the purposes of this Guide a food handler is any member of staff who prepares food directly, serves open foods, replenishes displays, or handles food even where packaged such as a checkout operator.

Legal requirement	Guide to compliance	Advice on good practice
Chapter X 1 *The proprietor of a food business shall ensure that food handlers engaged in the food business are supervised and instructed and/or trained in food hygiene matters commensurate with their work activities.*	This regulation introduces a requirement that food handlers be given supervision and instruction and/or training. The type of supervision and instruction and/or training that is required to be given however is dependant on the degree of product handling and on the nature of the product. A warehouseman who only handles sealed boxes of high risk foods still needs to know about for example, the importance of temperature control, stock rotation and pest control. A confectioner who sells and handles low risk sweets does not present the same risk as someone selling delicatessen products. It is important to note that there is however a <u>minimum</u> base level of hygiene awareness that is necessary even for the lowest risk category food handler.	

Legal requirement	Guide to compliance	Advice on good practice

Chapter X 1

Knowledge of basic hygiene principles and required practices is essential and instruction or training must be given to <u>all</u> food handlers providing them with a basic understanding before they start work. In determining training needs an employee's current knowledge and skills can be taken into account particularly where this can be demonstrated by possession of a suitable training course certificate.

The basic level of hygiene awareness necessary must encompass:

- Personal Hygiene standards including reporting of illness.

- Awareness of food hazards associated with the business and in particular the three hazards described in Part 2 of this Guide.

- Pest control awareness (i.e. recognising the signs).

- How to store food correctly including where required, the importance of temperature control.

The instruction or training must be appropriate to the job to be conducted, and may be either written or verbal.

For many individuals in a retail business (e.g. checkout operators or replenishers who are not handling open food directly) this level of awareness will be sufficient, provided they are then supervised to ensure they are working correctly.

In determining whether further instruction or training is necessary regard must be given to both the type of food and the way it is handled.

All persons carrying out food preparation, open food handlers for high and medium risk foods (see Part 3), and staff who may carry out a number of different tasks which include the above, will require further instruction or training. This will encompass for example, butchers, bakers and delicatessen counter staff.

Legal requirement	Guide to compliance	Advice on good practice

Chapter X 1

Such further instruction or training must, as a minimum include the following:-

● Basic food microbiology, including causes and prevention of food poisoning.

● Food storage and the importance of temperature control.

● Safe food preparation and handling practices, including prevention of contamination (if relevant).

● Personal hygiene.

● Cleaning procedures, use of equipment and handling of waste.

● Pest control - preventative measures.

Newly trained staff must be monitored shortly after training to ensure it has been understood.

Where temporary staff are provided, they may be able to demonstrate suitable knowledge. The proprietor must satisfy themselves that the temporary staff have such knowledge or otherwise assume they are untrained.

Where temporary staff are able to demonstrate appropriate levels of training it is recommended that they are still provided with brief instruction on the particular business and identified hazards and are supervised initially to verify skills.

All managers and supervisors of food handlers should have knowledge equal to or above that of their staff who are handling food. In this way management decisions can be consistent with good hygiene practices.

Managers and supervisors should also ensure visitors, workmen etc. are adequately informed of hygiene requirements and the possible consequences of their actions.

Chapter X 1

Timing

As stated above, a basic level of hygiene awareness must be provided for <u>all</u> food handlers before they start work.

For food handlers requiring further instruction or training, this must be completed as soon as practicable after commencing employment, with careful supervision and specific instruction being given in the interim.

It is important that supervision and instruction and/or training is seen not as a once and for all requirement but is re-assessed whenever changes are made to operations, practices or the categories of food handled.

Such food handlers should receive the further instructions or training within 12 weeks of commencing employment, with priority given to food handlers in the highest risk groups.

Recording and Evaluating

It is recommended that you keep a written record of all training activity undertaken by all members of staff. This will aid planning of future needs and indicate the level of skills and knowledge achieved by each individual, identifying any re-training requirements necessary. This exercise will also help you to demonstrate your compliance with the Regulations.

Additionally the knowledge and skills of staff should be occasionally reviewed to establish whether instruction or training has been successful or if further action is still needed. For small and medium sized businesses this can generally be done by informal supervision, though for larger businesses it is recommended that a more structured approach is adopted.

BACKGROUND INFORMATION

Where to obtain external training if required

Training formats or the medium used to deliver the training will be the choice of the retailer. Various options are available:

- Colleges, schools and some Environmental Health Departments run formal courses or can provide material. These often use a syllabus set by one of the following organisations.

    - Chartered Institute of Environmental Health
    - Royal Environmental Heath Institute of Scotland
    - Royal Institute of Public Health and Hygiene
    - Royal Society of Health
    - Society of Food Hygiene Technology

    Their addresses and telephone numbers appear in Appendix V. They can provide details of local courses or organisations.

- Consultants can be hired to train all employees within a business.

- Distance/open learning packages can be obtained via professional magazines or journals, or contact your local Environmental Health Department for information of availability of such packages.

- Suitable hygiene training may be provided as part of another wider vocational course, e.g. for catering or as part of an NVQ.

SUPERVISION AND INSTRUCTION AND/OR TRAINING CHECK LIST

This check list has been prepared to help you to judge whether you are complying with the requirements of this section. Whilst it is recommended that you complete it as shown, you are not obliged to do so under the Regulations.

		YES	NO	COMMENTS
1.	Are all food handlers provided with hygiene awareness knowledge at the start of their employment?	❑	❑	
2.	Is the knowledge of temporary staff assessed?	❑	❑	
3.	Is appropriate supervision provided for low risk food handlers?	❑	❑	
4.	Have all existing staff received the necessary essential supervision and instruction and/or training which is the recommended level for the type of food handling being carried out?	❑	❑	
5.	Is further training for higher risk food handlers completed as soon as practicable after employment commences?	❑	❑	
6.	Are skill and knowledge levels of staff monitored after further training?	❑	❑	
7.	Are training needs revised when jobs change?	❑	❑	

Some questions may not be applicable to your particular business and you can if you wish note this in the comments.

If the answer to all questions is Yes (or not applicable) then the requirements of this section will have been met. If any questions are answered No, comments should be written alongside and improvements necessary should be entered on the assessment chart.

Introduction

Pests are animals, birds or insects which live in or on food and either directly damage it or contaminate it. Whilst damage itself is serious, many pests are carriers of bacteria which can contaminate foods and cause illness. Pests also contaminate foods with hair, nesting materials, urine or faeces or even their bodies.

Pest Control

In order for pests to present a hazard to foods, they must have:

- Walked, flown or been carried into the premises.

- Found suitable places to live (and reproduce).

- Have access to warmth, suitable foods and in most cases, to water.

Pest control is founded upon managing these three areas by preventing access, denying harbourage and access to food and by destruction or eradication of any pests present.

Legal requirement	Guide to compliance	Advice on good practice
Chapter I 2 *The layout, design, construction and size of food premises shall ....*	**Exclusion or Preventing Access (Proofing)** - Buildings must be in good repair and condition in order to restrict pest access and help to eliminate potential breeding sites.	Wire mesh screens should be used to proof air bricks and ventilation panels. Made of stainless steel and with gaps no greater than 6 mm they will keep out mice. Holes, drain openings and other places where pests are likely to gain access should be sealed.
c) permit good food hygiene practices, including protection against cross contamination between and during operations, by .... external sources of contamination such as pests;	If windows open directly into food preparation areas <u>and</u> are used for ventilation when food is being prepared, then they must be fitted with screens if there is a risk of infestation or of contamination.	Screens should be capable of resisting the common flying insects and should have apertures of 2mm square or less.

Legal requirement	Guide to compliance	Advice on good practice
Chapter I 2	External doors should be kept closed when not in use and be well fitted to restrict access by pests. In food rooms where food is prepared, treated or processed and external doors have to be opened in warm weather for ventilation, screens must be fitted to keep insects and birds out.	The use of rubber or bristle strips can help proofing.
	Domestic pets must on no account be admitted to areas where open food is kept or handled. Assistance dogs are permitted provided access does not pose a risk of contamination of food.	
	Restriction by Denying Harbourage and Food Sources - The availability of food and refuse, together with a source of water, encourages pests to harbour and infestations to develop.	Do not stack goods against walls and in corners, which could create places where debris can build up to provide refuge for pests.
	It is obvious commercial sense to use oldest stocks first. This helps preventative pest control too, by never allowing any potential centre of infestation to remain undisturbed and undetected for long.	Ideally, mark stacking areas with painted lines on floor, allowing space around each stack for sweeping, floor washing and inspection.
	Waste food must not be allowed to build up so that it acts as an attraction for pests.	
	Many pests, especially rats, need drinking water. Deny them this and they will go elsewhere. Make sure that access to cisterns is barred. Repair dripping taps. Ensure that staff empty wash basins. Flies will breed rapidly in residues that have become wet through leaks or poor drainage.	Whilst proprietors of businesses can do much to prevent pest infestations by denying access and harbourage, it may be worth considering engaging a specialist pest control contractor who will advise on precautions to be taken as well as dealing with infestation. EHOs may also advise you on pest precautions.
	Traps and gratings must be kept clean and disinfected frequently to prevent flies using accumulated decomposing residues as a breeding site.	
	The premises must be periodically visually checked for signs of pest presence.	In larger premises an inspection schedule may be helpful. A record of this can be kept.

Legal requirement	Guide to compliance	Advice on good practice

Chapter IX 3

Adequate procedures must be in place to ensure pests are controlled.

Destruction or Eradication - Where pest infestations do occur these must be dealt with immediately. Treatments with chemicals, physical or biological agents must be carried out in such a way that they do not pose a threat to the safety or suitability of food.

Continuous destruction of flying insects can be achieved using electric fly traps with ultra-violet lamps. Manufacturers' instructions on their location, cleaning and replacement of lamps should be followed.

Where used, baits must be clearly identified and dated and kept away from foodstuffs that could be contaminated.

It is good practice to use electric fly traps in premises where open foods are displayed prominently, such as bakers' and butchers' shops.

Traditional fly papers, sprays or vapour killers are not suitable where open food is kept or handled.

Open grain baits should be avoided.

BACKGROUND INFORMATION

The Main Pest Groups

In seeking to control pests it is necessary to know your enemy - their appearance, habits and tell - tale signs of their presence.

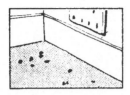

Droppings

Gnawing Damage

Gnawing Damage

Pest themselves

Increased number
of flies in the trap

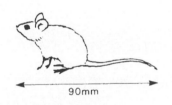

90mm

MOUSE

The brown rat and house mouse are the main rodent pest species. Like all rodents they have a pair of incisor teeth in both upper and lower jaws that continue to grow throughout life. To keep them at the correct length they gnaw on most hard materials, so apart from damaging raw materials, packaging and finished foods they also cause damage to the fabric of buildings, to electric wiring and plumbing. A mouse can enter a gap as small as 9mm.

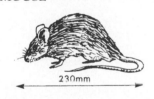

230mm

RAT

Their high reproductive ability can result in rapid increases in rodent populations and, under favourable conditions, rats and mice are capable of breeding throughout the year.

Being nocturnal creatures, cockroaches are seldom seen and consequently are not thought of as common British insects, but in recent years much attention has been focused on those species that share many of our buildings because of their real risk as carriers of disease organisms.

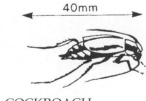

40mm

COCKROACH

The Oriental cockroach is now the most common cockroach in the UK. It can live outdoors in rubbish tips and in drains during warmer parts of the year as well as deep-seated harbourages inside, such as cellars and inside cavity walls. The second most common is the smaller, light brown German cockroach, which prefers warm and humid areas such as below sink units and inside the warm motor compartments of refrigerators.

BACKGROUND INFORMATION

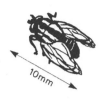

HOUSE FLY

There are many species of flies in the UK, but the most troublesome are house flies and blow flies, which are invariably contaminated with food-poisoning bacteria. Their feeding habits involve spitting on foods and they also transfer germs via their bodies. They can re-produce very rapidly and in warm weather the life cycle of egg, larva ('maggot'), to adult can be completed in just over a week!

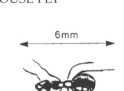

ANT

The garden ant or common black ant lives both outdoors and indoors, nesting in cracked paving, under stones, in rockeries, among plant roots and in sub-floor cavities. Ants have an acute sense of smell and quickly find out and infest exposed foods of every kind.

FLOUR BEETLE

Some beetles and moths are commonly associated with the stored or processed commodities in which they feed. Species of mite present similar infestation problems. Some live on specific foods to which they adapt, e.g. grain weevils on whole cereals, whilst others live on a wide variety of foods e.g., biscuit beetles. Damage is caused by both the larval and adult stages of beetles and mites, but by the larval stage only of moths.

Pest Birds

These are mainly the feral pigeon, house sparrow and starling. They cause problems particularly in warehouses but also indirectly by:-

- Providing nests which become breeding sites for many types of insects and mites, which may then move down into buildings.

- Building nests which can cause blockages to drains and gutters and ventilation.

- Spoiling foodstuffs with their droppings (which probably contains pathogens), feathers and also pecking open bagged goods.

- Fouling and defacing buildings.

PEST CONTROL CHECK LIST

This check list has been prepared to help you to judge whether you are complying with the requirements of this section. Whilst it is recommended that you complete it as shown, you are not obliged to do so under the Regulations.

	YES	NO	COMMENTS
1. Are all staff able to recognise potential pest problems in order to report them as they may occur?	☐	☐	
2. Are all external doors kept closed when not in use?	☐	☐	
3. Where necessary are openable windows to food preparation areas protected with fly screens?	☐	☐	
4. Is the building in good repair and condition to restrict pest access.	☐	☐	
5. Is waste food controlled so as not to act as an attraction for the pests.	☐	☐	
6. If provided, are electric fly traps properly positioned and regularly cleaned?	☐	☐	
7. Are domestic animals excluded from food areas?	☐	☐	

Some questions may not be applicable to your particular business and you can if you wish note this in the comments.

If the answer to all questions is Yes (or not applicable) then the requirements of this section will have been met. If any questions are answered No, comments should be written alongside and improvements necessary should be entered on the assessment chart.

Introduction

The provision and maintenance of the correct equipment, facilities and services in a food retail business occupies a key position in controlling the hazards of microbiological and physical contamination.

This section of the Guide deals with these aspects of the business premises in turn. It does not cover matters relating to the basic fabric of the premises which are dealt with in the following section on Structure.

SOME REQUIREMENTS OF THIS SECTION APPLY ONLY TO FOOD ROOMS - WHERE FOOD IS PREPARED, TREATED OR PROCESSED AND THIS IS SHOWN AT THE TOP OF EACH RELEVANT PAGE.

Equipment

Legal requirement	Guide to compliance	Advice on good practice
Chapter V 1		
All articles, fittings and equipment with which food comes into contact shall be kept clean and -	To enable effective cleaning food contact surfaces will need to be smooth, free from pits, crevices and chips.	
a) be so constructed, be of such materials, and be kept in such good order, repair and condition, as to minimise any risk of contamination of the food;	Materials must be readily cleanable, non-toxic and resistant to corrosion. Stainless steel is an ideal material and food grade plastics are generally suitable. Ceramics and enamelled ware are acceptable but care needs to be taken to avoid chipping. Heat resistant glassware is suitable for containers but ordinary glass may not be suitable, depending on risk of breakage.	
b) with the exception of non-returnable containers and packaging, be so constructed, be of such materials, and be kept in such good order, repair and condition, as to enable them to be kept thoroughly cleaned and, where necessary, disinfected, sufficient for the purposes intended;	Equipment must be constructed and kept in a state of good repair to reduce the risk of contamination from foreign bodies and lubricants and designed to facilitate cleaning. Regular cleaning of equipment is required, with disinfection of those items that come into direct contact with high risk foods.	Articles, fittings and equipment should be constructed to eliminate harbourage areas for debris. It is good practice to use only purpose made equipment - domestic equipment will often be unable to withstand sufficiently the handling, cleaning etc. in retail use.
c) be installed in such a manner as to allow adequate cleaning of the surrounding area.	Care must be taken in the installation of equipment such as slicers, mixers and refrigerators so that they do not become dirt traps. Sufficient space must be allowed around non-movable equipment to allow cleaning.	Heavy equipment is best provided with wheels/slides.

Specific Requirements for Food Rooms

Legal requirement	Guide to compliance	Advice on good practice
Chapter II 1 *(f) surfaces (including surfaces of equipment) in contact with food must be maintained in a sound condition and be easy to clean and, where necessary, disinfect. This will require the use of ....washable and non-toxic materials, unless the proprietor of the food business can satisfy the food authority that other materials used are appropriate.*	It is particularly important that surfaces which are regularly in direct contact with open foods such as chopping boards, tabletops, trays and utensils are made of suitable materials. The requirement also applies to internal parts of refrigerators or display cabinets. Stainless steel is an ideal food contact surface. Food-grade plastics are widely used and are particularly useful for utensils such as spoons, containers and for cutting boards. Ceramics and enamel ware are suitable provided they are treated with care and cease to be used if they become seriously chipped or pitted. Heat resistant glass is often used for display trays, dividers and fronts of cabinets and is readily cleaned and disinfected. Plastic laminates are suitable for work surfaces but will deteriorate if used for cutting. Stone and mineral composites are acceptable if non-porous and undamaged. Wooden food contact surfaces can retain moisture and are easily damaged and generally are not a suitable material. Wooden cutting boards in good condition can be used, but not for high risk foods. Purpose made butchers blocks for cutting raw meat only are suitable if cleaned properly and kept in good repair. Equipment must be regularly inspected and if found to be damaged such that it inhibits cleaning or poses a physical contamination hazard, should cease to be used. Scuffs and abrasions and similar wear and tear would not generally render equipment unsuitable for use if kept clean.	Areas in close proximity to food contact surfaces should be kept clean and well maintained if contamination may be transferred. Galvanised metals and ordinary steel are not ideal unless specially protected. It is good practice to avoid using self-adhesive plastic sheet for work surfaces. Wooden food contact surfaces are best avoided. Old disused equipment should be removed from the area to avoid accidental re-use.

Specific Requirements for Food Rooms

Facilities

Legal requirement	Guide to compliance	Advice on good practice
Chapter II 2 *Where necessary, adequate facilities must be provided for the cleaning and disinfecting of work tools and equipment. These facilities must be constructed of materials resistant to corrosion and must be easy to clean and have an adequate supply of hot and cold water.*	In most cases it will be necessary to provide a sink or machine to clean work tools and equipment. In some cases it may be possible however, to provide sufficient clean tools and equipment or remove soiled items to a separate area/premises for cleaning. All food contact equipment and tools will require periodic cleaning dependent on their usage. Work surfaces and some equipment can be cleaned in-situ though in other cases it will be necessary to provide a sink. This must be large enough to clean commonly used containers, trays or chopping boards. Sinks must be of corrosion-resistant materials e.g. stainless steel, ceramics, plastic or mineral composites. Sinks must be provided with enough hot and cold (potable) water to enable all cleaning operations to be carried out. Draining and/or drying facilities must be provided.	It is useful to have a double-bowl sink for cleaning and disinfecting. Dishwashing machines may be beneficial where a considerable amount of equipment needs to be cleaned. Dishwashers that operate at over 80°C reduce the need for disinfection. Air drying is particularly suitable where high temperature washing or rinsing is used. Re-usable cloths for drying present a contamination hazard and should be used on one work occasion only before laundering. Disposable paper towels are preferable.
Chapter II 3 *Where appropriate, adequate provision must be made for any necessary washing of the food. Every sink or other such facility provided for the washing of food must have an adequate supply of hot and/or cold potable water as required, and be kept clean.*	Where food needs to be washed sinks used for equipment washing can be used. If this practice is to be followed, the sinks must be thoroughly cleaned after each different use. If sinks are used frequently for washing food or if fresh fish is washed, it is recommended that separate sinks should be provided. Cold water supplies must be potable if used for washing food. Hot water is not required for food washing.	Signs can be provided to show what sinks are to be used for.

Legal requirement	Guide to compliance	Advice on good practice
Chapter I 3 *An adequate number of washbasins must be available, suitably located and designated for cleaning hands.*	The number and location of washbasins will be determined by the type of business, size of premise and numbers of staff employed. The principal guiding factor should be that a basin should always be readily available for use. For small premises one basin will generally be sufficient. Basins must be provided close to sanitary conveniences. Where high risk open foods are handled a basin must be available for that area. Basins must be positioned so that they are readily accessible. Handwash basins must not be used for washing food or equipment.	Basins should be positioned away from corners and ideally near the entrance of a food area to encourage usage. Handwash basins should be marked 'for handwashing only' or similar.
Chapter I 4 *Washbasins for cleaning hands must be provided with hot and cold (or appropriately mixed) running water, materials for cleaning hands and for hygienic drying. Where necessary, the provision for washing food must be separate from the hand washing facility.*	Basins must be provided with hot and cold water either from separate taps or alternatively via a single mixer tap. A supply of soap or detergent must be available. Hand drying can be achieved using paper towels, roller towels in cabinets or hot air dryers.	Where a mixed supply is provided, e.g. from a separate heating unit a temperature of approximately 50 °C is recommended. It is good practice to use a bactericidal detergent in a dispenser or provide disinfectant wipes for use after washing where high risk foods are handled. The use of ordinary fabric towels that are used more than once should be avoided. Bins should be provided for soiled disposable towels for where they are used.
Chapter 1 3 *An adequate number of flush lavatories must be available and connected to an effective drainage system.*	The number of lavatories provided depends upon the number of employees and is regulated by the Workplace (Health, Safety and Welfare) Regulations 1992. Lavatories must be connected to an effective drainage system through traps.	

Legal requirement	Guide to compliance	Advice on good practice
Chapter I 3 *Lavatories must not lead directly into rooms in which food is handled.*	Lavatories must be sited away from any food handling areas but if this is not possible there must be at least an intervening space between, with doors fitted at each side.	Intervening spaces should be ventilated. Doors to lavatories should be self closing.
Chapter I 9 *Adequate changing facilities for personnel must be provided where necessary.*	Where it is necessary for staff to wear protective clothing, this must be stored in a clean area away from areas where food is handled. If staff need to remove their everyday clothes, a suitable changing area must be provided.	Where a changing area is provided it is good practice to provide staff with individual lockers or cupboards to keep their clothing/belongings.

Services

Legal requirement	Guide to compliance	Advice on good practice
Chapter I 5 *There must be suitable and sufficient means of natural or mechanical ventilation.* *Mechanical air flow from a contaminated area to a clean area must be avoided. Ventilation systems must be so constructed as to enable filters and other parts requiring cleaning or replacement to be readily accessible.*	Ventilation is important to prevent the build up of heat, steam or dust, to reduce the risk of contamination of food from condensation and to remove odours which might affect the suitability of foods. For many small premises, natural ventilation provided by openable windows will be sufficient. Some older premises may have been built with few openings or be converted from buildings with little natural ventilation. In these cases or where the size of the premises or nature of operations conducted mean that natural ventilation is insufficient, mechanical means are likely to be needed. The simplest systems include openable ventilators or wall/window mounted fans. These must be placed as close as possible to the source of steam/fumes. Where air is drawn into clean areas, the location of air intakes should be carefully chosen to avoid the risks of taking in dust, dirt or odours or fumes from heaters. If fitted, screens/filters must be placed so as to facilitate removal and/or cleaning.	Screens/filters for mechanical ventilation should be provided wherever air is supplied to open food areas.

Legal requirement	Guide to compliance	Advice on good practice

Chapter I 6

All sanitary conveniences within food premises shall be provided with adequate natural or mechanical ventilation.

In the majority of premises, conveniences will be provided with openable windows. In other cases sufficient mechanical ventilation must be installed so as to ensure there is no build up of odours or humidity. Air from conveniences should be vented away from other windows/ventilation intakes.

Chapter I 7

Food premises must have adequate natural and/or artificial lighting.

Lighting must be sufficient for food handlers to work in a hygienic manner and to be readily able to see whether areas are clean and to detect signs of pests.

It is unlikely that natural lighting will be sufficient to supply all areas of a premise throughout the year; and artificial lighting will need to be provided.

Where artificial lighting is provided it should be positioned so as to avoid as far as possible glare or strong shadows.

Levels of illumination are measured in lux. The following levels are recommended:-

Food preparation areas - 500 lux at worktop level.

Retail sales areas - 500 lux.

Conveniences and changing rooms - 300 lux.

Store rooms - not less than 150 lux at floor level.

It is recommended that flush lighting is used to facilitate cleaning. Light fittings in open food areas or in display cabinets should be enclosed to prevent contamination of food in the event of breakage.

Chapter VII 1

There must be an adequate supply of potable water. This potable water must be used whenever necessary to ensure foodstuffs are not contaminated.

Water from the mains supply in the U.K. can be assumed to be potable. Supplies from private wells or other services must, unless checked, only be used for purposes which could not contaminate food, e.g. flushing lavatories or in closed heating systems.

Where water softeners or filters are used they should be maintained in good condition so that they do not contaminate the water.

Legal requirement	Guide to compliance	Advice on good practice
	Potable water must be used for inclusion into foods, washing food or hands, cleaning equipment and cleaning food contact surfaces. In larger premises storage tanks are often provided to ensure sufficient supplies. These must be securely covered. Any tanks for potable water must be maintained in good condition and comply with local Bye-laws.	
Chapter VII 2 *Where appropriate, ice must be made from potable water. This ice must be used whenever necessary to ensure foodstuffs are not contaminated. It must be made, handled and stored under conditions which protect it from all contamination.*	Any ice which is to be used in foods, or with which foods will come into contact must be made from potable water. Ice making machines must be cleaned regularly and periodically disinfected, in accordance with the manufacturers' instructions. Utensils used with ice must not become brittle when cold.	Utensils used with ice should be brightly coloured.
Chapter VII 3 *Steam used directly in contact with food must not contain any substance which presents a hazard to health, or is likely to contaminate the product.*	If liable to come into contact with food steam must be generated from potable water.	
Chapter VII 4 *Water unfit for drinking used for the generation of steam, refrigeration, fire control and other similar purposes not relating to food, must be conducted in separate systems, readily identifiable and having no connection with, nor any possibility of reflux into, the potable water systems.*	Where a premises does use non-potable supplies - e.g. for fire fighting, outlets must show their use.	Pipework and valves for non-potable supplies should be coloured distinctively and outlets marked "not for drinking". Non-potable water should not be used in food preparation areas.

Legal requirement	Guide to compliance	Advice on good practice

Chapter I 8

Drainage facilities must be adequate for the purpose intended; they must be designed and constructed to avoid the risk of contamination of foodstuffs.

Drainage systems serving food premises must be capable of efficiently disposing of waste water and soil drainage, and must prevent the entry of foul air or effluent from the drainage system into food rooms.

The system has to be of sufficient size to cope with peak loads without choking or flooding.

All points of entry into the drainage system must be protected by effective traps. Where internal inspection chambers have to be installed inside food premises, they must be accessible, and they must be closed with a secured, sealed, airtight double cover. All open food must be removed from a food room when an inspection chamber is opened. Stack ventilation pipes must be carried through to the outside of the premises and be placed away from air intakes.

Internal inspection chambers should be avoided if possible.

Chapter I 2

The layout, design, construction and size of food premises shall -
....
(d) provide, where necessary, suitable temperature conditions for the hygienic processing and storage of products.

Products which are required to be stored in particular temperature conditions must be so kept. Preparation areas must avoid the build up of excessive heat. It may therefore be necessary to consider the use of ventilation or air-conditioning equipment, or of heaters to ensure proper temperature conditions are maintained throughout the year.

EQUIPMENT AND FACILITIES CHECK LIST

This check list has been prepared to help you to judge whether you are complying with the requirements of this section. Whilst it is recommended that you complete it as shown, you are not obliged to do so under the Regulations.

		YES	NO	COMMENTS
1.	Is all equipment, including work surfaces of suitable materials, in good repair and easy to clean?	☐	☐	
2.	Are there enough sinks provided for washing equipment, and are the sinks large enough to allow the equipment to be cleaned properly?	☐	☐	
3.	Does the amount of food which needs washing indicate that separate sinks are needed for this purpose and if so are these provided?	☐	☐	
4.	Are there enough hand wash basins available with soap and suitable means of drying hands?	☐	☐	
5.	Are supplies of hot and/or cold water provided as required?	☐	☐	
6.	Are there enough lavatories?	☐	☐	
7.	Are lavatories separated from food rooms?	☐	☐	
8.	Is the level of ventilation in lavatories sufficient to remove odours and reduce humidity?	☐	☐	
9.	Is potable water used where required?	☐	☐	
10.	Are the lighting levels sufficient for those working on the premises to do their job hygienically?	☐	☐	

Some of the questions may not be applicable to your particular business and you can if you wish note this in the comments.

If the answer to all questions is Yes (or not applicable) then the requirements of this section will have been met. If any questions are answered No, comments should be written alongside and improvements necessary should be entered on the assessment chart.

Introduction

The basic function of any structure in food hygiene terms, be it a room or a whole building in which food is stored, handled or displayed is to protect the food from the elements of nature, air and water-borne forms of contamination, and damage/contamination by people, animals, birds and insects.

SOME REQUIREMENTS OF THIS SECTION APPLY ONLY TO FOOD ROOMS - WHERE FOOD IS PREPARED, TREATED OR PROCESSED AND THIS IS SHOWN AT THE TOP OF EACH RELEVANT PAGE.

General Requirements

Legal requirement	Guide to compliance	Advice on good practice
Chapter I 1 *Food premises must be kept clean and maintained in good repair and condition.*	It is important to note that this general requirement does not necessarily apply to all parts of food premises. Many premises may have offices or living accommodation associated with them and these will not be covered. Wherever food is handled, stored, displayed or served it <u>will be</u> covered, although a distinction is made between standards of cleanliness in a preparation area and in a warehouse. The standard of cleanliness and repair will therefore vary depending upon e.g. the use for the part of the premises, type of food being dealt with and how the food is packed. However, even areas such as store rooms and changing areas should be free from accumulated dirt and waste and be in good condition so as to allow effective cleaning.	Periodic inspection of all areas of the premises will identify defects or cleaning needs. Where cleaning schedules are used, it is important to include high wall surfaces, ventilation ducts and storage areas.
Chapter I 2 *The layout, design, construction and size of food premises shall -* *(a) permit adequate cleaning and/or disinfection;* *(b) be such as to protect against the accumulation of dirt,*	The layout, design and size of the premises must ensure that access can be obtained to all internal parts of the structure that require cleaning. Suitable materials must be used for walls, floors etc. to facilitate cleaning. (Special requirements apply to areas where open food is handled) see below.	The use of entry mats will help keep floors clean. They should be changed/cleaned when soiled.

Legal requirement	Guide to compliance	Advice on good practice
Chapter I 2		
contact with toxic materials,	Provision must be made for safe storage of e.g. cleaning materials. Building structure materials must not pose a risk of contamination of foods with toxic substances. This provision does not in itself require the replacement of existing lead water pipes in good condition.	
the shedding of particles into food	The choice of materials and finishes is important. The layout and design must avoid situations where open foods are kept below areas that may produce particles.	It is worthwhile avoiding finishes which require high levels of maintenance.
and the formation of condensation or undesirable mould on surfaces;	The layout etc. of the premises must provide adequate ventilation to restrict the formation of condensation. In areas subject to condensation, enhanced cleaning is required to avoid mould growth	Broken damp courses or leaking gutters can also result in mould growth.
(c) permit good food hygiene practices, including protection against cross contamination between and during operations, by foodstuffs, equipment, materials,	Layout etc. must allow separation of open ready to eat foods from raw foods, and wherever possible for different preparation areas and equipment. Where separate areas are not possible, the layout must facilitate effective cleaning and disinfection between handling of the different food types.	Layout should assist in food being handled "flowing" from "dirty" or raw areas to "clean" or ready to eat ones. Layout of premises where food preparation is undertaken should assist temperature sensitive foods to be handled quickly. Layout of premises should avoid deliveries and refuse having to be taken through food preparation areas.
water,	Leaks in the fabric of the building or in water services can enable foods to be contaminated by water.	
air supply or personnel and external sources of contamination such as pests;	Care must be taken that air contaminated by dust, dirt or odours is not brought into food premises where open food is handled. The structure of the building must be suitably proofed against access by pests.	

Specific Requirements for Food Rooms

The following structural requirements apply only to areas where foods are prepared, treated or processed. In retail premises this would include the areas behind service counters such as delicatessens or butchery or where any food preparation or packing is conducted. The requirements do not relate to other areas such as storerooms or the public parts of the shop, or any area where only packaged food is handled.

Floors

Legal requirement	Guide to compliance	Advice on good practice
Chapter II 1 *In rooms where food is prepared, treated or processed ...* *(a) floor surfaces must be maintained in a sound condition and they must be easy to clean and, where necessary, disinfect. This will require the use of impervious, non-absorbent, washable and non-toxic materials, unless the proprietor of the food business can satisfy the food authority that other materials used are appropriate.*	Floors in retail premises are likely to be subject to a lot of mechanical wear, high point loading from equipment, shelving or racking placed on it, impact damage and attack by various cleaning agents. They therefore have to be sufficiently strong, hard and durable so that the surface remains intact and easy to clean. There are a wide range of floor surfaces available which are generally suitable, including ceramic tiles, terrazzo, vinyl, epoxy resin and natural minerals. Background information on materials available is shown below. Some materials rely on grouting or sealing to fill gaps. Where used, the floor should be occasionally inspected and any damage repaired.	It is helpful if work tables and equipment can be readily moved to allow thorough cleaning.
Where appropriate, floors must allow adequate surface drainage;	Floor drains will not be necessary unless floors are constantly wet.	Where areas are constantly wet or equipment has to be hosed clean drainage should be provided and floors sloped toward the drain.

Specific Requirements for Food Rooms

Walls

Legal requirement	Guide to compliance	Advice on good practice
Chapter II 1 *(b) wall surfaces must be maintained in a sound condition and they must be easy to clean and, where necessary, disinfect. This will require the use of impervious, non-absorbent, washable and non-toxic materials and require a smooth surface up to a height appropriate for the operations, unless the proprietor of the food business can satisfy the food authority that other materials used are appropriate;*	Walls must be finished in a manner which enables them to be easy to clean up to a height where they would be liable to become soiled. Any damage or deterioration of the wall surface will inhibit or prevent cleaning and disinfection, allowing the build up of dirt and provide a breeding ground for pests and bacteria. Any loose, flaking or powdery material caused either by damage or general deterioration of the wall surface or coating could become a contamination risk to a product and must be removed and the area repaired as soon as possible. Suitable wall surfaces include ceramic tiles, washable painted plaster or rendering, fibre glass, plastic cladding, plastic coated fibre or chip board, metal sheeting, or epoxy resin coating. Often different materials will be used at low and high level.	It is recommended that suitable wall finishes are provided 0.5m above any adjacent work surface. Where there is a likelihood of damage extra protection should be provided in the form of barriers, posts or metal cladding. Ledges, ridges and recesses should be avoided wherever possible, as these may harbour dirt and provide unwanted storage areas. Wall floor junctions should be covered where possible to assist in cleaning.

Specific Requirements for Food Rooms

Ceilings and Other Fixtures and Fittings

Legal requirement	Guide to compliance	Advice on good practice
Chapter II 1 *(c) ceilings and overhead fixtures must be designed, constructed and finished to prevent the accumulation of dirt and reduce condensation, the growth of undesirable moulds and the shedding of particles;*	The inner surface of the roof structure will provide an acceptable surface e.g. pre-cast concrete, corrugated metal cladding, wood, provided it is kept clean and does not shed particles. Alternatively a fixed ceiling of painted plaster, or plastic panelling or similar can be used.	Overhead fixtures should be kept to a minimum. Where suspended ceilings are used services can be installed above them. Suspended ceilings can help to reduce condensation if used with proper ventilation but where employed they should be readily de-mountable for cleaning. Polystyrene or acoustic tiles are not readily cleanable and should not be used where open food is handled.
Chapter II 1 *(d) windows and other openings must be constructed to prevent the accumulation of dirt. Those which can be opened to the outside environment must where necessary be fitted with insect-proof screens which can be easily removed for cleaning. Where open windows would result in contamination of foodstuffs, windows must remain closed and fixed during production;*	Contamination via open windows is most likely to be wind blown debris and dust, or unpleasant odours and fumes either from traffic or adjacent premises. Whether this presents a risk of contamination will depend on whether the food is open or wrapped/packaged, and the type of food. High fat foods will be more likely to become tainted by unpleasant odours. If a risk of contamination is present, windows must be kept closed and alternative ventilation used. Insect screening of the windows is dealt with in the pest control section. (4.8)	Internal window ledges should be angled to prevent the accumulation of dirt.
Chapter II 1 *(e) doors must be easy to clean and, where necessary, disinfect. This will require the use of smooth and non-absorbent surfaces, unless the proprietor of the food business can satisfy the food authority that other materials used are appropriate;*	Doors can be made of the following materials:- toughened or laminated glass, metal (normally steel), wood which has either been painted with a gloss paint, or the surface sealed and water proofed with a wood stain or varnish; plastic, rubber or panelling. Handles and push plates, where fitted, must be readily cleanable and resistant to disinfectants.	Flush fitting doors reduce the opportunity for dirt build up. Doors with push plates are preferable to those with traditional knobs or handles

BACKGROUND INFORMATION

Materials for Floors

Ceramic Tiles

Tiles are either glazed or unglazed (quarry tiles). Tiles should be laid flat on a sand screed surface and waterproof grout should be used. The grout should be brought nearly level with the top of the tile to provide a smooth surface. Where a lip or ridge is created, an angled metal strip should be fitted to prevent the edge of the tile being chipped and to allow any wheeled unit to move across the floor smoothly.

Tiles are suitable for all areas though in frequently wet areas quarry tiles should be avoided. Any damaged or cracked tiles can be easily replaced. The presence of liquids including water on them can make them slippery so attention is required to remove liquid spillages or water from cleaning.

Terrazzo Tiles

These consist of marble chips embedded in cement. The top of the tile is polished smooth and the grout comes level with it to produce a completely smooth floor.

Terrazzo is easily attacked by chemicals and must be cleaned using a neutral detergent. Spillages of alkali or acid products should be removed as soon as possible, as prolonged contact will discolour/bleach and then damage the surface of the floor. The resistance of the floor to attack can be increased by treating with a chemical hardener or sealant after laying. Terrazzo is widely used for shop floors and preparation rooms because of its attractive appearance, range of colours and smooth easy clean surface.

Vinyl Tiles/Sheet

These materials are cheap, easy to lay, relatively hard wearing, easy to replace and easy to clean. The appearance and life of the floor can be enhanced by sealing with a polish or sealant. In heavy traffic areas, particularly where trolleys or wheeled cages are used, the surface can be damaged. Very hot items will damage the surface.

Concrete

Cheap and easy to lay. Provided the surface is sealed with a concrete hardener or an epoxy resin floor paint, a durable, smooth, easy cleanable surface is produced. If the surface of the concrete is not sealed it will dust, stain easily and be attacked by acids, alkalis and running water, and in these conditions the surface will then break up.

Sealed concrete is most suitable for warehouses and corridors and for sales floors. It can be used in preparation areas if in good condition and well sealed.

Epoxy Resin

This provides a smooth, continuous, attractive and easy to clean surface, which is resistant to impact damage, water, acid and alkalis.

Epoxy resin is expensive and normally has to be laid by contractors. The area has to be well ventilated whilst the floor dries and cures. Suitable for all areas, it is usually only used, however, for wet preparation areas.

Natural Minerals

Although rarely used today, in the past slate, granite and marble slabs have been used for floors. Provided they are in good condition, well grouted and can still be cleaned there is no need to replace them.

Wood

Often used in older premises, especially in store rooms. Provided the floor is without gaps, is in good condition and can be cleaned, there is no reason to replace it. Wood is not an ideal material for preparation areas but provided they are not particularly wet and the wood has been well sealed with varnish then it is acceptable.

BACKGROUND INFORMATION

Materials for Walls

Ceramic Tiles

Although tiles can be used in all areas, because of their cost they would normally only be used where open food is handled or displayed.

Painted Plaster or Rendering

A washable paint such as vinyl silk or gloss should be used to cover the surface. Cheap and easy to maintain. Widely used, it is often the standard finish provided to buildings. Generally acceptable though it is not recommended for use next to work surfaces or behind moveable equipment.

Plastic Cladding

Available in large sheets, easy to install it produces a light, bright easy to clean surface which is relatively inexpensive and is resistant to damage.

Although suitable for all areas apart from where there is a direct heat source, it is normally used where open food is handled, prepared or displayed.

Plastic Coated Fibre or Chip Board

Available in large sheets and easy to install. Produces an easy to clean surface, is relatively inexpensive and is resistant to minor impact damage.

Normally mounted on wooden battens, the void behind can harbour infestation. If the surface is damaged the underlying fibre or chipboard is exposed which is uncleanable.

Can be used in most areas provided the surface is not subject to impact damage. Should not be used in areas of high humidity or where condensation would occur.

Insulated Panelling

The panelling consists of plastic coated metal outer skins with insulating material sandwiched in between. Produces a light, bright, easy to clean surface, which is resistant to impact damage. Has excellent insulating properties.

The panelling is expensive and has to be installed by professional contractors. Suitable especially for temperature controlled preparation areas.

Metal Sheeting

Normally stainless steel or aluminium is used. Very resistant to heat, damage, abrasion and harsh cleaning techniques. Easy to clean.

Normally only used where there is very high risk of damage or where there is a direct heat surface e.g. around cooking equipment, especially where there is a naked flame.

Epoxy Resin Coating

This thin film/coating can be applied over a number of surfaces e.g. brick, breeze block, tiles or plaster to provide a smooth, continuous seamless coating which is easy to clean and resistant to minor impact damage.

Often used to improve old buildings as an alternative to cladding. Suitable for all areas, but not widely used.

Wood

Widely used in older buildings. Gradually being replaced as premises are refurbished/modernised. Provided it is in good condition and the surface is sealed either by varnish or paint to produce a smooth, cleanable surface which is maintained in good condition, there is no need to replace it.

STRUCTURE CHECK LIST

This check list has been prepared to help you to judge whether you are complying with the requirements of this section. Whilst it is recommended that you complete it as shown, you are not obliged to do so under the Regulations.

		YES	NO	COMMENTS
1.	Does the layout, design, construction and size permit adequate cleaning?	☐	☐	
2.	Are the materials used for the structure such as to avoid contamination of food?	☐	☐	
3.	Does the layout etc. facilitate effective separation of raw and ready to eat foods?	☐	☐	
4.	In food rooms are floors and walls of suitable material and in good condition for the operations undertaken?	☐	☐	
5.	Are suitable ceilings used in food rooms?	☐	☐	
6.	If openable windows to food rooms pose a risk of contamination are they kept closed when preparation of foods is being conducted?	☐	☐	
7.	Are doors to or in food rooms of suitable materials and easy to clean?	☐	☐	

Some of the questions may not be applicable to your particular business and you can if you wish note this in the comments.

If the answer to all questions is Yes (or not applicable) then the requirements of this section will have been met. If any questions are answered No, comments should be written alongside and improvements necessary should be entered on the assessment chart.

Introduction

Much of this Guide recommends action to be taken or procedures to be adopted to ensure the requirements of the Regulations are met. There is little value in only doing this as a one-off exercise and it is essential that a degree of monitoring is done to ensure that standards are maintained. In this context monitoring comprises both checks to be conducted on a regular basis to ensure individual controls are operating satisfactorily and also a periodic review of the system <u>as a whole</u> to verify it is still appropriate. Recommendations on the first type of monitoring have been included in the relevant sections and in this section guidance is given on the need for periodic reviews.

Monitoring

Legal requirement	Guide to compliance	Advice on good practice
Regulation 4 (3) *A proprietor of a food business shall .... ensure that adequate safety procedures are identified, implemented, maintained and reviewed on the basis of the following principles......* *(d) identification and implementation of effective control and monitoring procedures at those critical points; and* *(e) review of the analysis of food hazards, the critical points and the control and monitoring procedures periodically, and whenever the food business's operations change.*	Throughout the Guide specific recommendations for monitoring of particular activities are made. Suggested methods and frequencies must be followed or equivalent alternative methods adopted. It is essential that the assessment conducted under the hazard analysis requirements of the Regulations is kept up to date. The assessment must be repeated periodically and when any substantial change is made in products handled or practices followed, including for example:- ● starting to sell open or high risk foods; ● beginning preparation or production of foods; ● re-design or extension of premises. If any changes are limited to only one aspect of the business then it is acceptable to review this area only. In addition to the above, a review of the assessment conducted under the Regulations must be made occasionally to check that it is still satisfactory. The frequency of the review will depend on the size, nature and business conducted at any premises.	Small premises should conduct a full review every 3 years whilst large shops should do so more frequently. It is not expected that a review more than once per year will be required, provided no substantial changes are made.

Record Keeping

The Regulations do not require the keeping of any records. There are areas however where keeping records may be beneficial and the suggestions below are provided therefore as advice on good practice.

Legal requirement	Guide to compliance	Advice on good practice
THERE IS NO LEGAL REQUIREMENT IN THE REGULATIONS TO KEEP RECORDS	Whilst the Regulations do not require record keeping, other laws that could apply to your business may do.	It is recommended that for all premises, some written records are maintained. These will both help to ensure systems are being followed and also enable the business to demonstrate to an EHO what is being done. It is not necessary to set up a complex system - a simple record which is well understood is more beneficial. Records are not an end in themselves and the information shown should be used to assist control. It is recommended that the assessment chart in Part 3 of this Guide is completed and retained. Additionally it is suggested that records are kept for:- Temperature Checks (4.1, 4.2) Stock Rotation (4.3) Training (4.7) Cleaning (4.4) Pest Control (4.8) In order to assist you, Appendix III provides examples of suitable record sheets which you can freely copy or alter as desired.

MONITORING AND RECORDS CHECK LIST

This check list has been prepared to help you to judge whether you are complying with the requirements of this section. Whilst it is recommended that you complete it as shown, you are not obliged to do so under the Regulations.

	YES	NO	COMMENTS

1. Is monitoring of control measures conducted? ☐ ☐

2. Is the general assessment of risks reviewed periodically and when significant changes are made? ☐ ☐

If the answer to questions 1 and 2 is Yes then the requirements of this section will have been met. If either question is answered No, comments should be written alongside and improvements necessary should be entered on the assessment chart.

The remaining questions can be used to test adherence to good practice advice.

3. Are copies of the Assessment Charts in Part 3 completed and retained? ☐ ☐

4. Where other records are kept do they cover at least:
   Temperature Control
   Stock Rotation
   Training
   Cleaning
   Pest Control ☐ ☐

5. Where records are kept, are they checked routinely by management to ensure they are completed properly, kept up to date, and the information used? ☐ ☐

6. Where records are kept, are all appropriate staff aware of their responsibilities to complete written records on a regular basis as required? ☐ ☐

Introduction

For the purpose of this Guide, waste can be regarded as any item of food, ingredients, packaging materials, soiled cleaning cloths etc. which are not suitable for further use and which are intended to be disposed of. This includes any material which is to be recycled such as returnable bottles.

Waste needs to be controlled carefully since it presents a risk of physical contamination of foods intended for sale. Additionally, foods which are damaged, out of code or rotting, or are themselves contaminated, or food contact materials may present a risk of microbiological cross-contamination.

Legal requirement	Guide to compliance	Advice on good practice
Chapter VI 1 *Food waste and other refuse must not be allowed to accumulate in food rooms, except so far as is unavoidable for the proper functioning of the business.*	Food waste should be removed regularly from areas where it is produced or placed in containers provided for the purpose. Sufficient containers should be provided to readily accommodate the quantity of food waste ordinarily produced and positioned conveniently for the points where the waste occurs. In food rooms, containers need not be lidded if they are in frequent use and are regularly emptied. They must be readily cleanable and be disinfected periodically or disposable, and be clearly labelled or identified if there is any risk of confusion with other containers. Large refuse items such as boxes, crates, tins etc. must be removed from the food room as soon as practicable.	Particular care should be taken to remove waste from slicing machines, food preparation surfaces after work periods and at the end of the day. The use of colour-coded containers is recommended. Where refuse bags are used they should be distinct from any other similar bags. Where wet waste is produced lining containers with plastic bags is good practice.
Chapter VI 2 *Food waste and other refuse must be deposited in closeable containers unless the proprietor of the food business can satisfy the food authority that other types of containers used are appropriate. These containers must be of an appropriate construction, kept in sound condition, and where necessary be easy to clean and disinfect.*	Once food waste is removed from food rooms it must be placed in a lidded, tied or sealed container. Other food waste including damaged or out of code product to be disposed of and refuse must be deposited in closeable containers. These must be made of readily cleanable materials such as plastics or metal and not be so damaged as to be insecure or leak. Refuse such as cardboard, clean packing materials, paper or other uncontaminated wrappings intended for re-cycling need not be placed in closed containers provided they are so separated and dealt with so as not to pose a risk of contamination to foods.	

Legal requirement	Guide to compliance	Advice on good practice
Chapter VI 2 (cont)	Food items that are not for sale but are intended to be returned to a supplier/depot must be kept in a designated area, but if in secure packaging, need not be placed in closeable containers.	
Chapter VI 3		
Adequate provision must be made for the removal and storage of food waste and other refuse. Refuse stores must be designed and managed in such a way as to enable them to be kept clean, and to protect against access by pests, and against contamination of food, drinking water, equipment or premises.	A defined area must be allotted for the storage of waste pending disposal. If this is inside the premises it must be away from food rooms and be readily cleanable.

Care must be taken to ensure waste or materials for re-cycling do not act as an attraction to pests. Where e.g. foxes, birds or cats are liable to forage in waste areas then closed stores, fencing etc. should be provided.

Where stores provide facilities for re-cycling which are available for the public, the area must be kept clean, and have suitable containers which are regularly emptied. | The storage area for waste should not be sited immediately adjacent to entrances or windows to food rooms.

It is good practice to store waste on a hard area that can be readily cleaned down.

Waste should not be permitted to cause litter in the surrounding area or, if liquid, to leak into drains or streams.

Public re-cycling facilities should be sited away from entrances and open windows of the store. |

Disposal of Waste

In most cases disposal by the local authority refuse service will be satisfactory. All authorities have special arrangements for the collection of trade waste and it is advisable to establish what these are. As an alternative, many contractors are prepared to collect waste and dispose of it but in this case further requirements apply.

The Environment Protection Act 1990 (EPA) imposes a "duty of care" on businesses to ensure any waste is appropriately disposed of. Any contractor who collects waste is required to be licensed by the Environment Agency and you should ask for and keep a copy of the licence if you intend to use a contractor.

Transfer Notes

Regulations under the EPA require anyone collecting and disposing of waste to have a transfer note which accompanies the waste throughout its journey. Note that a transfer note is specific for each premises. The transfer note will show:-

- The address of the business where waste is collected
- A general description of the waste
- The type of container (e.g. bag, skip, wheelie bin)
- Collection frequency.

You must advise the contractor if any changes to the type of waste are made.

Transfer notes must be retained for a period of 2 years after expiry.

The Environment Agency will provide further advice on waste disposal.

WASTE DISPOSAL CHECK LIST

This check list has been prepared to help you to judge whether you are complying with the requirements of this section. Whilst it is recommended that you complete it as shown, you are not obliged to do so under the Regulations.

		YES	NO	COMMENTS
1.	Are sufficient bins etc. provided for food waste in food rooms and conveniently positioned?	☐	☐	
2.	In food rooms are waste bins washable and lidded if not regularly emptied?	☐	☐	
3.	Is waste removed from food rooms at least daily?	☐	☐	
4.	Is all waste clearly identifiable as such?	☐	☐	
5.	Is waste placed in a designated area, and if inside, away from food rooms?	☐	☐	
6.	Are employees aware of their responsibilities concerning waste?	☐	☐	
7.	Is waste awaiting disposal placed in closed containers (except for materials to be re-cycled)?	☐	☐	

Some of the questions may not be applicable to your particular business and you can if you wish note this in the comments.

If the answer to all questions is Yes (or not applicable) then the requirements of this section will have been met. If any questions are answered No, comments should be written alongside and improvements necessary should be entered on the assessment chart.

Even the smallest business may become involved in a manufacturer's product recall, have to deal with products which are the subject of a customer complaint, or are affected by the consequences of a fire, flood or breakdown of refrigeration equipment.

Product Recall

The Regulations refer in several places to the need to protect food from contamination and to avoid selling foods which are so affected. This section deals with the specific problems of product withdrawal or recall and **advice given is for good practice.**

Suppliers may for several reasons issue instructions to retailers to withdraw a product. There may be a problem with the packaging or labelling or the recall may be caused by the discovery of contaminated product or deliberate tampering. It is essential that in the event of a recall, any instructions are followed quickly and if required, items are removed from sale.

There may be occasions when a retailer would need to institute a product recall on their own behalf. The British Retail Consortium have issued guidelines on Product Recall which should be followed.

If the recall relates to product which is not pre-packed e.g. fresh meat, it is essential to be able to trace the affected items. The use of code control records (see 4.3) will assist here.

You may also receive information from a customer or EHO that a customer has been taken ill after consuming food from your shop. In these circumstances you will need to identify the product concerned and possibly remove it from sale.

Any withdrawn product should be clearly identified as not being for sale, separated from other foods and if not pre-packed be placed in secured containers.

Other Emergencies

Business may be affected by other emergencies such as fires, floods or refrigeration equipment breakdown which may affect the safety or wholesomeness of foods. In each case proprietors should:-

- Separate product that may have been affected. Note: smoke and water damage may be more extensive than will be initially apparent and if in doubt consider products affected.

- Assess the affected product carefully taking account of the three main food safety hazards outlined in Part 2 of the Guide.

In some cases, e.g. for canned foods, the packaging will generally protect the product, whereas for open foods you should presume they have been affected.

For chilled and frozen foods, their safety and suitability for sale will depend on the temperature they have reached and the time they have been out of proper temperature control. We recommend that specialist advice is sought from an EHO.

- Carefully dispose of any product that cannot be sold in accordance with Section 4.12 .

In most cases businesses will have insurance cover for emergencies and the insurer should be contacted at the earliest opportunity. Many insurers provide assistance to businesses in such circumstances.

EMERGENCY PROCEDURES CHECK LIST

This check list has been prepared to help you to judge whether you are complying with the requirements of this section. Whilst it is recommended that you complete it as shown, you are not obliged to do so under the Regulations.

		YES	NO	COMMENTS
1)	Are proper code checking procedures in place to facilitate any recall?	☐	☐	
2)	Are staff aware of procedures to follow in the event of a recall?	☐	☐	
3)	Are recalled/withdrawn products kept separate from other foods?	☐	☐	
4)	For other emergencies are staff aware of the recommended procedures?	☐	☐	

Some of the questions may not be applicable to your particular business and you can if you wish note this in the comments.

If the answer to all questions is Yes (or not applicable) then the requirements of this section will have been met. If any questions are answered No, comments should be written alongside and improvements necessary should be entered on the assessment chart.

Introduction

Transport is an important facet of many retail businesses. The types of vehicles used will vary from dedicated vehicles owned and maintained by the retailer to general goods vans and open flat trucks used to transport such products as fresh produce from market to store.

The transporting of foodstuffs provides a significant opportunity for contamination and spoilage. Contamination can occur if foodstuffs are carried in dirty receptacles, are inadequately packaged or packaging is damaged due to improper handling. A further potential risk is introduced if the outside of food vehicles are allowed to become heavily soiled. Equally, consumers expect food vehicles to be clean!

Legal requirement	Guide to compliance	Advice on good practice
Chapter IV 1 *Conveyances and/or containers used for transporting foodstuffs must be kept clean and maintained in good repair and condition in order to protect foodstuffs from contamination, and must, where necessary, be designed and constructed to permit adequate cleaning and/or disinfection.*	The type of vehicle used must reflect the risk associated with the product being transported. It may be appropriate to carry fresh produce on an open flat bed truck, whilst carrying cut poultry in this way would be totally unacceptable. Vehicles used for transporting high risk, open foods must be enclosed and be capable of thorough cleaning and/or disinfection. Vehicles may need to be adapted so that they are suitable. If wet foods such as fish are to be transported then the interior of the vehicle may need to be capable of withstanding hosing with clean water. Containers used for transporting foods will include bags, boxes, crates, racks and purpose made transport trays. For open high risk foods, containers of plastic or metal or other material which is readily cleanable must be employed.	Family cars/estates should not be used to transport high risk foods but are suitable only for those which are fully enclosed/wrapped and require no temperature control e.g. canned foods, biscuits or soft drinks etc. Where significant transport of open foods is carried out it is recommended that purpose made containers be used. The use of colour coding for different types of product is good practice. Vehicle containers should be included in any cleaning programme.
Chapter IV 2 *(1) Receptacles in vehicles and/or containers must not be used for transporting anything other than foodstuffs where this may result in contamination of foodstuffs.*	Food containers must not be used for non-foodstuffs such as cleaning chemicals where there is a risk of contamination. There is no reason why they cannot be used for non-hazardous materials such as wrapping/packaging materials, provided they are cleaned out thoroughly before food use.	

Legal requirement	Guide to compliance	Advice on good practice
Chapter IV 3 *Where conveyances and/or containers are used for transporting anything in addition to foodstuffs or for transporting different foodstuffs at the same time, there must be effective separation of products, where necessary, to protect against the risk of contamination.*	Where goods are securely packaged in containers they may be transported together. Care must be taken when any open foods are being transported that they are separated and/or covered to prevent possible contamination.	
Chapter IV 4 *Where conveyances and/or containers have been used for transporting anything other than foodstuffs or for transporting different foodstuffs, there must be effective cleaning between loads to avoid the risk of contamination.*	The adequacy of cleaning will depend on what has been transported and what is to be carried next. If products such as fruit and vegetables, meat or fish are carried then thorough cleaning and disinfection of the vehicle or containers must be performed before high risk, ready to eat foods are carried, unless all foodstuffs are securely packaged.	
Chapter IV 5 *Foodstuffs in conveyances and/or containers must be so placed and protected as to minimise the risk of contamination.*	Fully wrapped/packaged foodstuffs will generally meet this requirement. Open foods must be carried in enclosed vehicles or covered containers. These must be sufficient to protect against dust/debris from the vehicles or container falling into the food or dirt/fumes from traffic contaminating the food. Fresh fruits and vegetables that have not been peeled or cut into pieces need not be carried in enclosed vehicles or covered containers.	It is good practice to treat fruit and vegetables as other foods.
Chapter IV 6 *Where necessary, conveyances and/or containers used for transporting foodstuffs, must be capable of maintaining foodstuffs at appropriate temperatures and, where necessary, designed to allow those temperatures to be monitored.*	The cold chain is only as good as the weakest link and that is often the transport element. The risk of temperature abuse leading to product spoilage is a very real hazard. When the products being transported are required to be sold in a chilled state at a particular temperature then it must be transported at that temperature in order to maintain the cold chain.	

Legal requirement	Guide to compliance	Advice on good practice
Chapter IV 6 (cont)	Chill cabinets used in the sales area for displays are <u>not</u> designed to reduce the temperature of foods which have been allowed to rise above the temperature intended for them. Specific temperature requirements vary for different types of perishable foods and specialist advice should be sought if required. For some journeys using insulated containers or vehicles may be sufficient but often mechanical or cryogenic cooling will be needed. The determining factor for the method used will be whether the specific legal requirements for the foods concerned can be maintained. For vehicles carrying frozen or chilled foods there must be a means of monitoring product temperature either directly, or indirectly by monitoring the air temperature. For example, on purpose built vehicles a thermometer will usually be provided though it must be remembered that the temperature shown may not represent temperature of the products themselves. (See also Page 33 re. delivery). There is no obligation under the Regulations to provide continuous temperature monitoring throughout a journey.	Product temperatures can be checked using hand held thermometers and the between pack method (See Appendix II) is recommended.
Chapter IV 2 *(2) Bulk foodstuffs in liquid, granulate or powder form must be transported in receptacles and/or containers/tankers reserved for the transport of foodstuffs if otherwise there is a risk of contamination. Such containers must be marked in a clearly visible and indelible fashion, in one or more Community languages, to show that they are used for the transport of foodstuffs, or must be marked "for foodstuffs only".*	This requirement will seldom apply to retailers. However in a few instances bulk foodstuffs may be delivered to retail premises e.g. flour. Retailers must check that any delivery is from a vehicle which meets this Regulation before acceptance.	Care should be taken when discharging bulk containers at retail level to ensure that contamination is not introduced by means of "dirty" valves/piping.

Food Safety (General Food Hygiene) Regulations 1995 – Guide to compliance by Retailers

TRANSPORT CHECK LIST

This check list has been prepared to help you to judge whether you are complying with the requirements of this section. Whilst it is recommended that you complete it as shown, you are not obliged to do so under the Regulations.

		YES	NO	COMMENTS
1.	Are vehicles/containers used for transporting food clean and in good repair?	☐	☐	
2.	Is adequate separation available to prevent contamination?	☐	☐	
3.	Are vehicles/containers effectively cleaned and/or disinfected between different uses?	☐	☐	
4.	Are open foods protected from dust, debris or fumes in transport?	☐	☐	
5.	Are appropriate temperatures maintained during transport?	☐	☐	
6.	Are there means of monitoring temperatures?	☐	☐	

Some of the questions may not be applicable to your particular business and you can if you wish note this in the comments.

If the answer to all questions is Yes (or not applicable) then the requirements of this section will have been met. If any questions are answered No, comments should be written alongside and improvements necessary should be entered on the assessment chart.

4.15   MOVABLE/ TEMPORARY PREMISES
PREMISES USED PRIMARILY AS A PRIVATE DWELLING

Introduction

Mobile retail premises include market stalls and vehicles built as, or converted for use as shops. Temporary premises typically cover church halls or stands at exhibitions. This section also applies to temporary stands, used for example for demonstrations or for food sampling within a store. Dwellings are seldom also used as shops. This section is not intended to apply to the domestic part of mixed premises, e.g. where a flat is provided over a retail shop, unless the dwelling area is used for food storage or preparation for the business. Essentially it is expected that equivalent standards to those employed in conventional shops will be followed and therefore advice given in relation to e.g. food handling or personal hygiene is equally appropriate. In other areas however the Regulations provide for the different circumstances for these special situations. Guidance is given below only where it differs from the main part of the Guide.

Legal requirement	Guide to compliance	Advice on good practice
Chapter III 1 *Premises .... shall be so sited, designed, constructed, and kept clean and maintained in good repair and condition, as to avoid the risk of contaminating foodstuffs and harbouring pests, so far as is reasonably practicable.*	The basic requirement is qualified here by the phrase 'so far as is reasonably practicable'. This will depend on the nature of the premises and the type of foods sold. In determining what is reasonably practicable regard must be given to the costs and difficulties of following a particular course, compared with the risk of not doing so. Traditional practice may be used as a guide, provided such practices have not been shown to pose a risk to consumers.	
Chapter III 2 *In particular and where necessary -* *(a) appropriate facilities must be available to maintain adequate personal hygiene (including facilities for the hygienic washing and drying of hands, hygienic sanitary arrangements and changing facilities);*	If only pre-packed food is being sold, it is not necessary to provide handwashing or sanitary facilities at the premises. Where open food is handled a washbasin or bowls specifically for handwashing must be provided with a means of hand drying. (See 4.9)	Bactericidal soap is recommended

Legal requirement	Guide to compliance	Advice on good practice

Chapter III 2

(b) surfaces in contact with food must be in a sound condition and be easy to clean and, where necessary, disinfect. This will require the use of smooth, washable, non-toxic materials, unless the proprietor of the food business can satisfy the food authority that other materials used are appropriate;

For temporary premises and stalls it is acceptable to use plastic sheets or impervious cloths which would ordinarily be inadequately robust. They must nevertheless be in clean and good condition.

(c) adequate provision must be made for the cleaning and, where necessary, disinfecting of work utensils and equipment;

See Section 4.9. The use of bowls instead of fixed facilities is sufficient.

As an alternative to providing cleaning facilities, an adequate supply of clean utensils can be provided, soiled utensils being regularly replaced. Dirty utensils or equipment can be returned to permanent premises for cleaning. This is unlikely to be satisfactory for operations which involve significant open food handling.

(d) adequate provision must be made for the cleaning of foodstuffs;

Where required, follow the advice in the main part of the Guide (see 4.9), but using bowls instead of sinks is sufficient. Where a single sink is available it must be cleaned between different uses.

(e) an adequate supply of hot and/or cold potable water must be available;

Where a piped supply is unavailable, suitable containers filled with potable water will suffice. If it is necessary to wash utensils or equipment, hot water must be available.

(f) adequate arrangements and/or facilities for the hygienic storage and disposal of hazardous and/or inedible substances and waste (whether liquid or solid) must be available;

Many temporary or domestic premises will be connected to mains drainage. Where this is not provided liquid waste must be fed to suitable containers for later disposal. Other waste must be placed in suitable bags or containers (see 4.12). For stalls etc. it is unacceptable to allow waste to flow or fall onto the ground. Special provisions may be made in fixed markets.

Legislation	Guide to Compliance	Advice on good practice
Chapter III 2		
(g) adequate facilities and/or arrangements for maintaining and monitoring suitable food temperature conditions must be available;	Where foods are required to be kept below a particular temperature, insulated containers or ice packs can be used but in warm weather proper refrigeration equipment will probably be needed where foods are displayed for more than 4 hours. Similarly, special equipment is likely to be required to meet hot holding temperature requirements of 63ºC or above. A means of monitoring temperatures must be provided.	It is good practice not to have on display more chilled foods than is strictly necessary.
(h) foodstuffs must be so placed as to avoid, so far as is reasonably practicable, the risk of contamination.	The general requirements of the rest of this Guide will apply. For market stalls etc. foods will usually be exposed to a greater degree than in a conventional outlet and this is acceptable provided methods used have not been shown to pose a risk to consumers. Care must be taken to place open food so that it will not be brushed by passers-by or animals.	It is advised that preparation of foods be minimised in mobile/temporary, or domestic premises. The use of barriers or screens to protect exposed foods from contact or contamination by customers is recommended. Fruits and vegetables should not be stored on the floor in yards or on pavement areas.

Food Safety (General Food Hygiene) Regulations 1995 – Guide to compliance by Retailers

MOVABLE/TEMPORARY PREMISES CHECK LIST

This check list has been prepared to help you to judge whether you are complying with the requirements of this section. Whilst it is recommended that you complete it as shown, you are not obliged to do so under the Regulations.

		YES	NO	COMMENTS
1.	Are facilities available to ensure adequate personal hygiene?	☐	☐	
2.	Are food contact surfaces of sound condition and easily cleanable?	☐	☐	
3.	Are clean utensils and equipment used?	☐	☐	
4.	Is hot and/or cold potable water available?	☐	☐	
5.	Are there adequate arrangements made to dispose of waste?	☐	☐	
6.	Are there facilities to maintain and monitor temperature where necessary?	☐	☐	
7.	Are foods placed/displayed so as to avoid, as far as is practicable, contamination?	☐	☐	

Some of the questions may not be applicable to your particular business and you can if you wish note this in the comments.

If the answer to all questions is Yes (or not applicable) then the requirements of this section will have been met. If any questions are answered No, comments should be written alongside and improvements necessary should be entered on the assessment chart.

Some retailers may have vending machines on their premises. These will usually be for fully packaged foods such as confectionery or canned drinks. Where foods are prepared for sale from a vending machine on retail premises, the advice given elsewhere in this Guide must be followed in relation to the food preparation.

Legal requirement	Guide to compliance	Advice on good practice
Chapter III 1 *vending machines shall be so sited, designed, constructed, and kept clean and maintained in good repair and condition, as to avoid the risk of contaminating foodstuffs and harbouring pests, so far as is reasonably practicable.*	Retailers have no influence over the design and construction of vending machines. The machine must be kept clean and manufacturer's instructions followed. Machines must be sited so that maintenance staff and cleaners have ready access. The area around vending machines must be kept clean. Chapter III 2 which sets out how the requirements of the Regulations apply to both temporary premises (see 4.15) and vending machines is qualified by the words "where necessary". In retail premises the majority of vending machines are likely to be for the sale of prepacked low risk foodstuffs such as canned drinks/ confectionery. In these cases no additional requirements to those above are necessary.	A regular maintenance contract with the supplier is recommended. Bins for customer use should be provided.
Chapter III 2 *(e) An adequate supply of hot and/or cold potable water must be available;*	Machines will ordinarily be connected to mains supplies. If containers of water are used these must be from potable supplies.	

VENDING MACHINE CHECK LIST

This check list has been prepared to help you to judge whether you are complying with the requirements of this section. Whilst it is recommended that you complete it as shown, you are not obliged to do so under the Regulations.

	YES	NO	COMMENTS
1. Are manufacturer's instructions regarding installation, cleaning and maintenance followed?	❑	❑	
2. Is the area around the vending machine maintained in a clean and tidy condition?	❑	❑	
3. Are water supplies to vending machines from potable sources?	❑	❑	
4. If products for sale in vending machines are prepared on site, are the relevant standards in the rest of the Guide met?	❑	❑	

Some of the questions may not be applicable to your particular business and you can if you wish note this in the comments.

If the answer to all questions is Yes (or not applicable) then the requirements of this section will have been met. If any questions are answered No, comments should be written alongside and improvements necessary should be entered on the assessment chart.

BACKGROUND INFORMATION

APPENDIX I

OFFICIAL INSPECTIONS OF FOOD PREMISES

Introduction

The purpose of this Appendix is to provide background information on the role of inspectors, their powers and the way that they should deal with your business. It is not part of the Industry Guide to Good Hygiene Practice.

Official inspections of food businesses are conducted by Enforcement Officers who are officials of the Local Authority. They will generally be either:-

    i)   Environmental Health Officers (EHOs)
    ii)   Trading Standards Officers (TSOs)
    iii)   Other Local Authority Officers eg food safety, technical or sampling officers

Both EHOs and TSOs enforce aspects of the Food Safety Act 1990 and the organisation of their respective work differs across the country. EHOs and other Officers from the Environmental Health Department are responsible for food safety and hygiene issues including compliance with The Food Safety (General Food Hygiene) Regulations, whilst TSOs deal with matters relating to food composition, labelling and misleading claims. In certain regions of the country including London, Scotland, Northern Ireland and some Metropolitan Boroughs of England EHOs are additionally responsible for food composition, labelling and misleading claims.

Inspections

Enforcement Officers have wide powers to enter business premises at any reasonable time, to examine goods, equipment and documentation and to take samples of food or materials. It is an offence to obstruct Officers from carrying out their duties.

You will probably come into contact with Enforcement Officers when they visit your premises to conduct a programmed routine inspection, or perhaps if they have received a complaint from a customer.

It is a requirement that all food premises are registered with the Local Authority. From this information the Enforcement Officer will draw up a list of premises and determine the frequency that each will be visited, according to the risk posed. Low risk premises such as newsagents/confectioners may only be inspected once every five years, whilst retailers such as delicatessens or supermarkets will be visited perhaps annually. Inspection frequencies will be varied as necessary to take account of foods sold, practices and inspection or complaint history.

When an Enforcement Officer visits your premises you should adopt the following procedure:-

- Ensure the Officer is met with courtesy and co-operation.

- Ask politely for their identity card.

- Establish the reason for the visit.

- Take note of their name, title, name of Local Authority, office address and telephone number.

- Ensure that before they leave you are clear as to what you should do or expect to happen. Many officers will provide a written note of their visit on request.

BACKGROUND INFORMATION

The way in which the Officers enforce the law may differ, and will depend upon:-

- Your past record of compliance and the risks associated with your business.

- The policies of the Local Authority.

- The standards of food hygiene in your premises at the time.

The above points will determine which form of action the Officer will take.

Enforcement Action

The different forms of action are:-

Verbal Advice

If there are no contraventions of the law, the Officer will not normally need to re-visit until the next programmed inspection. They may however offer informal advice on possible improvements. A written report of the inspection should be given/sent to you.

Advisory Letter

The officer will provide advice in writing if requested, or if contraventions of the law are found. When matters relate to contraventions, the Officer should ensure any letter contains information which will enable you to understand what work is necessary and why it is necessary, identify which Regulation has been contravened and detail the measures which in the opinion of the Officer are required to be taken in order to secure compliance. The Officer may also point out where you fail to follow this Guide even though compliance with this Guide is not mandatory. They should also make clear the differences between any matters which you are <u>required</u> to attend to and any that are simply advisory.

There may be a request to carry out any necessary works within a certain time period, and perhaps a statement that a re-visit will be made within a few months. If you disagree with some of the requests or do not understand why you are being asked to do them, contact the Officer about your queries. Do not wait for a re-visit before asking these questions, as they may suspect that you are being un-cooperative.

Improvement Notices

These are usually only used if there are contraventions <u>and</u> a poor previous record of non-compliance or where the Officer has reason to believe that an informal approach will be unsuccessful.

When an Officer decides that it is appropriate to serve an Improvement Notice, the Officer must first send the proprietor a "Minded to" Notice. This preliminary notice will give a specified period (Government suggests a minimum of 14 days) either to make written or oral representations to the authority about the proposed enforcement action before the Improvement Notice can be served. If the proprietor wishes to make oral representation they will need to contact the enforcement authority within a fixed period (again, the Government suggests minimum of 7 days) to arrange the necessary meeting. Whenever a business provides written or oral representations, the authority must take a fresh and fair look at the proposed action in the light of those representations. If it is decided that an Improvement Notice should not be issued then this will be confirmed in writing. If, however, the Officer remains of the view that an Improvement Notice is appropriate, a Notice will be issued.

A "Minded to" Notice details information similar to that contained in an Improvement Notice. It should be clearly headed "Minded to" Notice. It will contain information on the apparent breaches of Regulations, the reasons for the Officer considering the service of an Improvement Notice and details of the measures needed to comply. The "Minded to" Notice also details how much time would be provided on an Improvement Notice if it were subsequently served. Details of how to make oral or written representations, including any time restraints will be included.

BACKGROUND INFORMATION

Improvement notices themselves state the alleged legal contravention, the reason why the Officer is of that opinion, the steps you need to take to comply, and the date by which the work must be done. These are prescribed legal documents, and failure to carry out the required steps by the compliance date is a criminal offence. The maximum penalty is an unlimited fine or imprisonment for 2 years if the case is tried in the Crown Court. If the case is heard in the Magistrates Court the fines can be up to level 5 (currently £5,000) on each offence and/or imprisonment for 6 months. If you disagree with the notice, perhaps because it requires work that you feel is outside the law, operationally not feasible, or gives you insufficient time, contact the Officer and put across your reasons. The Officer may be persuaded to withdraw the notice, or vary it in your favour. The Officer should also be prepared to accept similar work to that on the notice if that remedies the contravention. If the Officer is unwilling to accept any of this, and you still believe the notice is wrong, you can appeal against the notice within 21 days of the date of service. You may need to seek legal advice from a solicitor, and/or your Trade Body. Remember that an appeal can incur legal costs, and so you might wish to exhaust your other options before appealing.

Emergency Prohibition Notices/Orders

If there are major contraventions which pose an imminent risk to health in your premises the Officer can issue you with an Emergency Prohibition Notice. Unlike Improvement Notices above, these notices come into immediate effect once you receive them. The notice could require the immediate closure of your premises, or the prevention of use of a piece of equipment or process. The Officer must apply to the local Magistrate (or Sheriff in Scotland) for an Emergency Prohibition Order within three days of serving the Emergency Prohibition Notice, if this is not done the Notice ceases to have effect. This procedure is designed to give Enforcement Officers the power to deal with very bad situations, but also requires the endorsement of the Courts to ensure that the Officer is acting reasonably. The Officer should only implement the Prohibition process if there is an "imminent risk to health". This means for example, if the condition of the premises appeared to carry a high risk of causing an outbreak of food poisoning within the next few days.

Prosecution

If serious breaches of law are discovered by an officer, they may decide to report the matter and the Local Authority may prosecute you. In Scotland all prosecutions are initiated and processed through the court by Procurators Fiscal acting in the public interest after consideration of reports and evidence submitted by Enforcement Officers. If found guilty you may be fined or in serious cases imprisoned. You can also be prohibited from running a food business.

The Officer will investigate the reasons for non-compliance and may caution you. If the Officer informs you that offences have been committed they must formally caution you before questioning you concerning the offences. The phrase generally used is "You do not have to say anything unless you wish to do so but it may harm your defence if you fail to mention anything when questioned that you later rely on in court". If you intend to seek legal advice then you should tell the Officer that you wish to do so before answering any questions after the caution.

In addition to the above actions the Officer has further specific powers.

Formal Caution

As an alternative to a prosecution a Local Authority in England, Wales and Northern Ireland, may choose instead, with your consent, to issue a "Formal Caution". (Note: this is totally different to the caution described above, issued during an investigation). A "Formal Caution" is an admission of an offence and may be brought to the Court's attention in the event of a subsequent prosecution if you are found guilty. Local Authorities will comply with a Code of Practice issued by the Home Office, which ensures you are given clear information should the need arise.

Sampling

Officers are empowered to take, or more usually, purchase samples of food, which are then sent for testing. In some cases the sample may be divided into portions by the Officer and sealed, and one portion left with you so you may if you wish have the sample tested yourself.

BACKGROUND INFORMATION

Seizure of Food

When an Officer finds food which they consider does not comply with food safety requirements then it may be seized. You should be given a receipt. The Officer has to obtain the permission of a Magistrate to destroy the food and you can attend to give your views. If the Magistrate does not agree with the Officer you may be entitled to compensation.

Seizure of other materials or documents/records

An Officer may take documents/records, books, point of sale material or equipment which is believed to be required as evidence.

Public Health Incident

In the event of an outbreak of food poisioning or food related infection, in addition to action by Enforcement Officers, your premises may be inspected by a Consultant in Communicable Disease Control (a doctor specialising in public health medicine) from the local Health Authority or Board.

Home Authority Principle

If you operate the same business from more than one premises, and these premises are located within different Local Authority boundaries, the following information applies.

If one of your premises is the main head office of your business, the Local Authority for the area in which it is located will usually act as your "Home Authority". This means that this particular Authority should deal with food safety matters highlighted by the Local Authorities responsible for your other outlets in the country and co-ordinate contacts with you.   They will also usually provide assistance to you in how to comply with the law.

Note.   Please bear in mind that operating The Home Authority principle does not replace the powers of Local Authorities who may still act independently in enforcing the legislation. The objective is improved consistency of enforcement.

BACKGROUND INFORMATION

APPENDIX II

TEMPERATURE MONITORING

The main problems with taking temperatures in retail cabinets are the choice of equipment and the necessity to have suitably trained staff available to conduct the checks.

It must be noted that the Regulations do not lay down how to take temperature readings and therefore, any equipment that gives an indication of the temperature at which a cabinet is operating is valid.

However, the products on sale will certainly be checked by the Enforcement Officer with accurate equipment and if the food is not at the correct temperature you may face prosecution.

Types of Thermometer

All thermometers have two key parts:-

i)   A sensor which gives the temperature of the place where it is located.

ii)   A reading scale or display.

In Place Simple Devices

The simplest devices are self-adhesive liquid crystal display strips and dial or digital thermometers built in to the cabinet.

These are generally adequate, but as they measure air temperature they only give an approximate indication of the product temperature.

Glass Thermometers

Because of the risk of breakage and contamination of foods these thermometers are not recommended where any open foods are handled.

Electronic Probe Thermometers

Of varying accuracy and expense. Must be calibrated and checked regularly. Hand-held probes of this type are used by most enforcement officers. A variety of sensor probes can be obtained for the one electronic unit. Some manufacturers now provide a hand-held unit with a number of plug-in sensors that can be fixed to monitor several cabinets.

Manufacturers' instructions on use should be followed.

Automatic Air Temperature Monitoring

A system that fits each cabinet with the appropriate number of sensors each wired back to a control box in an office. Temperatures are monitored continually and any deviation from fixed levels (allowing for defrost) usually sets off an alarm.

This system is really only suitable for larger premises and whilst initially expensive, provides constant monitoring and, usually, printed records.

Infra-Red Probes

These are relatively new devices, which enable rapid temperature measurements of product surfaces. These are best used for screening of product and care should be taken if using this method exclusively.

BACKGROUND INFORMATION

Methods of Temperature Recording

Before taking any temperature reading it is important to establish whether the cabinet operates an automatic defrost cycle. (Refer to manufacturer's instructions). If it does defrost automatically then it will usually do so at least once per day and readings taken within one hour of defrosting will not be reliable. Readings should not be made immediately after re-stocking.

Air Temperature

This may be carried out using a hand-held probe which is placed in the cabinet. By holding the probe at various points where the food is stacked a good approximation of cabinet or coldstore temperature can be established. Tests may have to be conducted to establish the correlation of air and product temperature or manufacturer's advice taken.

Placing the probe at the 'air off' point marked on Diagram A will give the temperature of the air coming off the refrigeration unit.

'Air on' gives the temperature of air returning from the cabinet to the refrigeration unit and will therefore represent the highest air temperature in the cabinet.

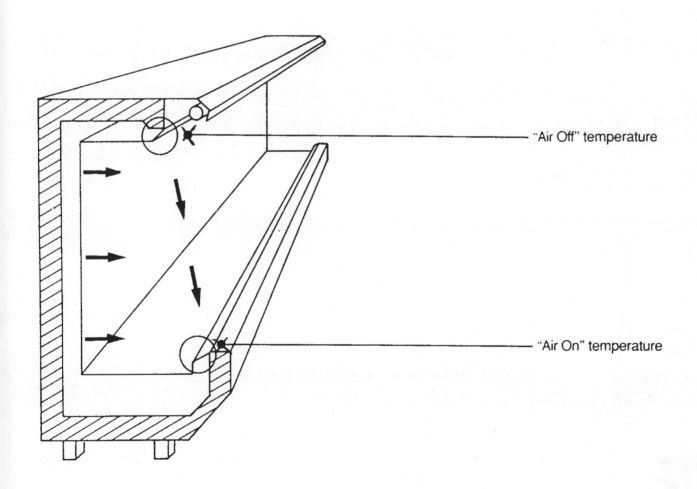

DIAGRAM A - AIR TEMPERATURE MEASUREMENT

BACKGROUND INFORMATION

Between pack temperature

This gives a good approximation of product temperature. A flattened or wire probe is held in close contact between two packs of food. (Diagram B)

It is important to select foods which give good contact and where packaging best allows the food temperature to be measured. Products should not be removed from the cabinet to measure.

Products should be measured along different shelves in each part of the cabinet and at different times of the day to establish the pattern of operation of each cabinet. Once this has been determined then choose a place within the cabinet to take daily readings that gives the best confidence that all the food products within the cabinet are being kept at the required temperature.

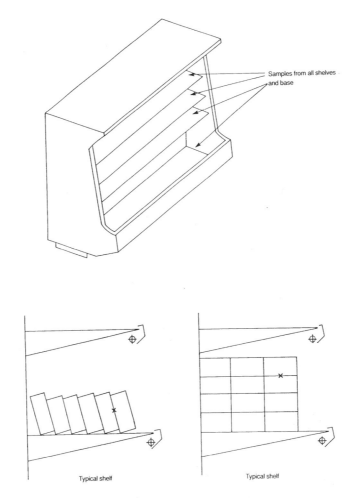

Samples from all shelves and base

Typical shelf   Typical shelf

X MARKS POSITION OF PROBE

DIAGRAM B - BETWEEN PACK TEMPERATURE MEASUREMENT

Direct Product Testing

This involves inserting a probe directly into the core of the product itself.   This method is particularly suitable for loose items such as cheeses and bulk displays but it is essential that the probe is cleaned and disinfected before use and between use on different products.

If this method is used for packaged product where the packaging is punctured, the product must be removed from sale and disposed of.

Food Safety (General Food Hygiene) Regulations 1995 – Guide to compliance by Retailers

APPENDIX III   - SUGGESTED FORMS FOR OPTIONAL RECORD KEEPING

TEMPERATURE CONTROL RECORD - DELIVERIES

Date: _____

Time	Delivery From	Lorry/Product Temperature (if applicable)	Checked by (Signature)	Accept	Reject	Reason for Rejection/ Action Taken

TRAINING RECORD

Name	Date	Task for which Training Completed	Signature of Trainee	Signature of Trainer

Food Safety (General Food Hygiene) Regulations 1995 – Guide to compliance by Retailers

CLEANING RECORD

Date: _____

Equipment/Area Cleaned	Time	Cleaning Equipment/Method	Carried out by (Signature)	Checked by (Signature)	Any Problems/Action Taken

PEST CONTROL RECORD

Date	Time	Area Checked for Infestation	Checked by (Signature)	Any Problems Noted and Action Taken

Food Safety (General Food Hygiene) Regulations 1995 – Guide to compliance by Retailers

STOCK ROTATION/CODE CHECK RECORD

Required Frequency of Check Daily/Weekly/Monthly*/other......
(* Delete as required)

Products to be Checked	Date Checked	Checked by (Signature)	Action Taken e.g. Price Reduction/Disposal

TEMPERATURE CONTROL RECORD - CABINETS/COLD STORES

Date: _____

Time	Cabinet/Coldstore	Required Temperature	Actual Air Temperature	Checked by (Signature)	Action Taken if not Required Temperature

APPENDIX IV

GLOSSARY

Glossary	Definition
Ambient Temperature	The temperature of the surrounding environment. Commonly used to mean room temperature.
Assistance Dogs	Specially trained dogs to help owners with visual, hearing or other disabilities.
Bacteria	Single celled living organisms. Some may spoil food and some may cause illness.
Bactericidal Soap	A soap/detergent containing ingredients that help to destroy bacteria present on hands.
Biological Agents	Means of pest control using other animals e.g. sparrowhawk for bird infestation.
Chillers/Coldstores	Equipment to keep food cool normally between 0°C and 8°C or frozen.
Cleaning	The removal of food residues, dirt, grease and other undesirable debris.
Compliance	Measures that satisfy the legal requirement.
Contamination	The introduction into the food of undesirable materials or micro-organisms, or of taint that may affect its safety or wholesomeness.
Core Temperature	The temperature found at the centre of the thickest part of a piece of food.
Coved	Rounded finish to the junctions between walls and floors, or between two walls to make cleaning easier.
Cross-Contamination	The transfer of micro-organisms (usually bacteria) from contaminated foods to other foods.
Cryogenic Cooling	A system of refrigeration using the injection of liquified gas into the storage chamber.
Defrost of Equipment	Periodic switching off of the refrigeration plant to allow ice build up on the evaporator to be removed.
Detergent	Cleaning agent for removal of grease and food residues.
Disinfection	Reduction in levels of contamination on food equipment or in food premises, normally by the use of chemicals to kill micro-organisms. Disinfectants used must be suitable for use in food premises.
Dormant	Description of bacteria in non-growing state but still alive ready to multiply when conditions are favourable.
EHO	Environmental Health Officer. Employed by a Local Authority. Enforces food safety (and sometimes food composition) legislation.
Electric Fly Killers	Equipment to control flies and other flying insects. Insects are attracted by UV lamps and destroyed on a high voltage grid or captured.
Fly Screen	Fine mesh screen fitted to windows and other openings to stop entry of flies and other insects.
Food	The definition of food includes drink and ice.
Food Handler	Anyone who handles or prepares food whether open (unwrapped) or packaged.
Food Poisoning	Illness transmitted by food. Caused either by infection or toxin.
Food Room	Part of a food premises where foodstuffs are prepared, treated or processed.

Glossary	Definition
Food Waste	Any food, including damaged goods, items which have exceeded their shelf life, trimmings or debris whether packaged or open and which are intended to be disposed of.
Foreign Object	Materials or substances from the environment or from food handlers that may contaminate the food.
Further Training	Training for a food handler in addition to Hygiene Awareness covering; basic food microbiology, food storage and the importance of temperature control, safe food preparation and handling practices, personal hygiene, cleaning procedures and handling of waste and pest control.
Harbourage	Areas in which pests can hide and/or nest because they are inaccessible to cleaning or inspection.
Hazard	Anything that may cause harm to a person who eats the food.
Hazard Analysis	A system which identifies food hazards, where they occur and the identification of measures to control them.
Hermetically sealed	A package for a foodstuff with an air-tight seal, e.g. a can.
High Risk Foods	Ready to eat foods. Foods that have already gone through most or all of their preparation steps. There will be a "high risk" if these are contaminated or allowed to deteriorate because there are no further preparation steps to control the hazard.
Hygiene	All measures to ensure the safety and wholesomeness of food.
Hygiene Awareness	Knowledge by a food handler of personal hygiene, food hazards and pest control awareness sufficient to enable them to commence work.
Infestation	Entry and survival of pest animals and insects in a premises or within equipment or products.
Legislation	Acts of Parliament, Regulations and European Community Regulations.
Load Lines	Levels marked on refrigerated units above which product will be out of refrigeration or obstruct the air flow resulting in a failure to be kept at the correct temperature.
Lux	A measure of light levels.
Micro-Organisms	Any small living organism especially bacteria, yeasts, moulds and viruses.
Mould	Micro-organism that can grow at low temperature in damp conditions even in high sugar/high salt food products. Spoilage organism usually clearly evident to the naked eye as grey/green substance.
Open Food	Food which is not fully wrapped.
Pathogenic Micro-Organisms	Micro-organism that can cause illness or harm.
Pests	Any unwanted animal that enters and may live in the premises or foodstuffs.
Potable Water	Water which meets legislative requirements as to its wholesomeness for drinking.
Preserved Foods	Foods processed, packed and stored in such a way that they will not allow the growth of micro-organisms which would result in spoilage or food poisoning.
Probe	Part of temperature measuring equipment that can be inserted between packs or into product to obtain temperature readings.
Product Codes	Date marking on product to show its safe display and user life within which the food should be consumed.
Product Life/Shelf Life	Length of time food can be stored or displayed while retaining its safety and wholesomeness.

Glossary	Definition
Proofing (against pests)	Design, construction and treatment of premises, doors, windows and entry points for services to restrict the entry of pests.
Protective Clothing	Coats, aprons, hats etc. to be worn by food handlers to prevent contamination of food products by the individual.
Refrigeration	All equipment used to keep food cool.
Relevant food	High risk foods as described in column A of assessment table 1 in Part 3 of this Guide, and other foods which are stated to require refrigeration at a specified temperature.
Sanitizer	Chemical for cleaning and disinfecting equipment or work surfaces.
Sneeze Guards	Screen, usually glass or other transparent material, fitted to some food display units. May reduce airborne contamination from customers sneezing or coughing.
Spoilage	Food deterioration resulting in off flavours, odours and possibly appearance indicating products are unsuitable for sale or to eat.
Sterilise	Treatment with heat or chemicals to kill <u>all</u> micro-organisms and viruses.
Stock Rotation	Practice of ensuring all stock is sold within shelf life.
Taint	Contamination of food with undesirable flavours or odours often from another product e.g. chocolate will develop a soapy flavour if stored next to detergent washing powders.
Thermometer	Equipment used to measure temperature of equipment or products.
Toxin	Poisonous substance. May be contamination from external sources e.g. chemical spillage or produced by growth of micro-organisms.
TSO	Trading Standards Officer - employed by a Local Authority. Enforces food composition (and sometimes hygiene) Regulations.
Use by Date	Date mark required on highly microbiologically perishable pre-packed foods. It is an offence to sell food after its "Use By" date.
Virus	Microscopic organism. Some are transmitted by foods and may cause illness. Viruses cannot multiply or grow on foods.
Waste	Any product, packaging or materials that are unwanted and intended to be disposed of and removed from a food area or premises.
Wholesome	Food fit to eat and free from defects

APPENDIX V

- British Retail Consortium
  5 Grafton Street
  London W1X 3LB
  Tel. No. 0171 647 1500
  Fax No. 0171 647 1599

- Anaphylaxis Campaign
  P O Box 149
  Fleet
  Hampshire GU13 9XU
  Tel No. 01252 542 029

- British Frozen Food Federation
  (For RFIC Guide on Storage and handling frozen food)
  3rd Floor
  Springfield House
  Springfield Road
  Grantham
  Lincolnshire NG31 7BG
  Tel No. 01476 515 300

- Chartered Institute of Environmental Health
  Chadwick Court
  15 Hatfields
  London SE1 8DJ
  Tel No. 0171 928 6006
  Fax No. 0171 261 1960

- Dept of Health Publications
  (For "Food Handlers Fitness to Work")
  P O Box 410
  Wetherby
  West Yorkshire
  LS23 7LN

- Dept of Health Publications
  Room 501A, Skipton House
  80 London Road
  London SE1 6LH
  Tel No. 0171 972 5071
  Fax No. 0171 972 5141

- Environment Agency
  Rio House
  Waterside Drive
  Aztec West
  Almondsbury
  Bristol BS12 4UD
  Tel No. 01454 624 400

- The Stationery Office Publications
  P O Box 276
  London
  SW8 5DT
  Tel No. 0171 873 9090

Contents

- Institute of Food Science and Technology
  5 Cambridge Court
  210 Shepherds Bush Road
  London W6 7NL
  Tel No. 0171 603 6316
  Fax No. 0171 602 9936

- LACOTS (Local Authorities Co-ordinating Body on Food and Trading Standards)
  P O Box 6
  1A Robert Street
  Croydon CR9 1LG
  Tel. No. 0181 688 1996
  Fax. No. 0181 680 1509

- Royal Environmental Health Institute of Scotland
  3 Manor Place
  Edinburgh EH3 7DH
  Tel. No. 0131 225 6999
  Fax No. 0131 225 3993

- Royal Institute of Public Health & Hygiene
  28 Portland Place
  London W1N 4DE
  Tel. No. 0171 580 2731

- Royal Society of Health
  38A St George's Drive
  London SW1V 4BH
  Tel. No. 0171 630 0121

- Society of Food Hygiene Technology
  P O Box 37
  Lymington
  Hants SO41 9WL
  Tel./Fax. No. 01590 671979

Your Local Enforcement Officer

Name ....

Address ....

Tel No ....

APPENDIX VI

INDEX TO THE REGULATIONS

Food Safety (General Food Hygiene) Regulations 1995

REGULATION		GUIDE	
NUMBER	**SUBJECT**	**PART/SECTION**	**PAGE**
Regulation 1	Citation and commencement date	Not included	
Regulation 2	Definitions and interpretation	Not included	
Regulation 3	Application of Regulations	Not included	
Regulation 4	Obligation upon Proprietors of food businesses	Part 2 Part 3 Section 4.11	4 7 86
Regulation 5	Persons suffering from certain medical conditions	Section 4.5	50
Regulation 6	Penalties and Offences	Not included	
Regulation 7	Applications	Not included	
Regulation 8	Enforcement	Not included	
Regulation 9	Amendments	Not included	
Regulation 10	Revocations	Not included	

Schedule 1

Chapter 1 General Requirements for food premises (other than those specified in Chapter III)			
Regulation		Guide	
Reference	Subject	Section	Page
Chapter I 1	Premises to be kept clean and in good repair	4.4 4.10	42 78
Chapter I 2	Layout, design, construction and size of premises	4.1 4.8 4.9 4.10	31 62, 63 76 78, 79
Chapter I 3	Wash hand basins and lavatories	4.9	71, 72
Chapter I 4	Handwashing and drying	4.9	71
Chapter I 5	Ventilation systems	4.9	73
Chapter I 6	Ventilation of sanitary conveniences	4.9	74
Chapter I 7	Lighting	4.9	74
Chapter I 8	Drainage	4.9	76
Chapter I 9	Changing facilities	4.9	72

Chapter II Specific requirements in rooms where foodstuffs are prepared, treated or processed (excluding dining areas and those premises specified in Chapter III)				
Regulation		Guide	
Reference	Subject	Section	Page
Chapter II 1	Floors	4.10	80
	Walls	4.10	81
	Ceilings	4.10	82
	Windows	4.10	82
	Doors	4.10	82
	Food contact surfaces	4.9	69
Chapter II 2	Facilities for cleaning of tools and equipment	4.9	70
Chapter II 3	Provision for washing of food	4.9	70

Chapter III Requirements for moveable and/or temporary premises (such as marquees, market stalls, mobile sales vehicles) premises used primarily as a private dwelling house, premises used occasionally for catering purposes and vending machines				
Regulation		Guide	
Reference	Subject	Section	Page
Chapter III 1	Precautions to avoid contamination and harbourage of pests	4.15 4.16	98 102
Chapter III 2	Personal Hygiene	4.15	98
	Food contact surfaces	4.15	99
	Cleaning of work utensils and equipment	4.15	99
	Cleaning of foodstuffs	4.15	99
	Water supply	4.15 4.16	99 102
	Waste disposal	4.15	99
	Temperature control	4.15	100
	Avoiding contamination	4.15	100

Chapter IV			
Transport			
Regulation		Guide	
Reference	Subject	Section	Page
Chapter IV 1	Conveyances and/or containers	4.14	94
Chapter IV 2	Receptacles in vehicles/containers Bulk foodstuffs	4.14 4.14	94 96
Chapter IV 3	Separation of products	4.14	95
Chapter IV 4	Cleaning between different loads	4.14	95
Chapter IV 5	Minimising contamination	4.14	95
Chapter IV 6	Temperature control	4.14	95, 96

Chapter V			
Equipment Requirements			
Regulation		Guide	
Reference	Subject	Section	Page
Chapter V 1	Equipment to be kept clean	4.4 4.9	42 68
	Minimise contamination	4.9	68
	Maintained in good condition	4.9	68
	Installed to allow cleaning of the surrounding area	4.9	68

Chapter VI			
Food Waste			
Regulation		Guide	
Reference	Subject	Section	Page
Chapter VI 1	Controlling of food waste	4.12	89
Chapter VI 2	Containers for food waste	4.12	89, 90
Chapter VI 3	Removal and storage of food waste	4.12	90

Chapter VII			
Water Supply			
Regulation		Guide	
Reference	Subject	Section	Page
Chapter VII 1	Adequate supply of potable water	4.9	74, 75
Chapter VII 2	Ice making	4.9	75
Chapter VII 3	Use of steam	4.9	75
Chapter VII 4	Control of water unfit for drinking	4.9	75

Chapter VIII Personal Hygiene			
Regulation		Guide	
Reference	Subject	Section	Page
Chapter VIII 1	Personal cleanliness and protective clothing	4.5	48, 49
Chapter VIII 2	Disease/infection of food handlers	4.5	50

Chapter IX Provisions applicable to Foodstuffs			
Regulation		Guide	
Reference	Subject	Section	Page
Chapter IX 1	Acceptance of raw materials	4.2	33
Chapter IX 2	Storage of raw materials	4.2	34
Chapter IX 3	Protection from contamination and pest control	4.2 4.3 4.6 4.8	35 38, 39 52, 53, 54 64
Chapter IX 4	Storage of Hazardous Substances	4.2	35

Chapter X Training			
Regulation		Guide	
Reference	Subject	Section	Page
Chapter X 1	Supervision, instruction and/or training	4.7	56-59

Schedule 2	Amendments	Not included
Schedule 3	Revocations	Not included

Food Safety (Temperature Control) Regulations 1995

REGULATION		GUIDE	
NUMBER	**SUBJECT**	**PART/SECTION**	**PAGE**
Regulation 1	Citation and commencement date	Not included	
Regulation 2	Interpretation	Not included	
Regulation 3	Application of Regulations	Not included	
Regulation 4	Chill holding requirements	4.1	16, 17
Regulation 5	General exemptions from chill holding requirements	4.1	17, 18, 19
Regulation 6	Temperatures set by manufacturers	4.1	19, 20
Regulation 7	Chill holding tolerance periods	4.1	20, 21
Regulation 8	Hot holding requirements	4.1	22
Regulation 9	Hot holding defences	4.1	22, 23
Regulation 10	Food which is a risk to health	4.1	15, 16
Regulation 11	Cooling of food	4.1	23
Regulation 12	Guides to good hygiene practice	4.1	24
Regulation 13	Chill and hot holding requirements in Scotland	4.1	26, 27
Regulation 14	Reheating of food in Scotland	4.1	28
Regulation 15	Treatment of gelatine in Scotland	4.1	29
Regulation 16	Food which is a risk to health in Scotland	4.1	25, 26
Regulation 17	Offences and Penalties	Not included	
Regulation 18	Applications of provisions of the Act	Not included	
Regulation 19	Enforcement and execution	Not included	
Regulation 20	Revocations	Not included	

Food Safety (General Food Hygiene) Regulations 1995 – Guide to compliance by Retailers